THE STERLI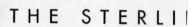

Buddha

and

HIS TEACHINGS

THE STERLING BOOK OF

Buddha

and

HIS TEACHINGS

Kingsley Heendeniya
MBBS (Cey.), DPH (Lond.)

NEW DAWN PRESS, INC.
UK • USA • INDIA

Dedicated
To
Ven. Ñānavira Thera
and
Ven. Ñānamoli Thera

NEW DAWN PRESS GROUP

Published by New Dawn Press Group

New Dawn Press, 2 Tintern Close, Slough, Berkshire, SL1-2TB, UK
e-mail: ndpuk@mail.newdawnpress.com

New Dawn Press, Inc., 244 South Randall Rd # 90, Elgin, IL 60123, USA
e-mail: sales@newdawnpress.com

New Dawn Press (An Imprint of Sterling Publishers (P) Ltd.)
A-59, Okhla Industrial Area, Phase-II, New Delhi-110020, INDIA
e-mail: info@sterlingpublishers.com
www.sterlingpublishers.com

Sole distributors in Sri Lanka, Singapore and Malaysia
Buddhist Cultural Centre
125 Anderson Road, Nedimala,
Dehiwala, Sri Lanka
Tel: + 94 11-2734256, 2728468, Fax: 2736737

The Sterling Book of: The Buddha and His Teachings
Copyright © 2004 by Kingsley Heendeniya
ISBN 1 84557 168 1

PRINTED IN INDIA

Contents

Chapter One

Aim and Scope of This Book

This book is written on the invitation of the publisher to complement their series of titles on the great religions that are extant today. My aim is to give an overview of the life and times of the Buddha – who does not need any introduction – and his teachings, in a planned collection of essays, to indicate particularly, as other books in this genre do not, *why he taught it*. The book will be sold worldwide and therefore, I shall limit esoteric words, omitting also diacritical marks, used scholarly for correct enunciation of Pali. The Buddha spoke Prakrit, a spoken dialect in northern India, now extinct. His teaching was written down in Sri Lanka in Pali, a precise language developed from it, used exclusively in the Dhamma. [The Dhamma is written also in Sanskrit, Chinese, Tibetan, Burmese, Thai, Korean, English, German, French etc.] I have included a list of useful Pali words with their diacritical marks.

The word *Dhamma* means 'the Teaching' and the portmanteau word *dhamma* is translated as 'things'. Another key word is '*dukkha*'. It is generally translated as 'suffering'. Throughout the book I shall be guided by the English translations of the Pali texts in the books published from the writings of two of the most renowned English monks of our time— both deceased—Venerable Nanavira Thera and Venerable Nanamoli Thera who I had the great fortune to meet and know. They came together to Sri Lanka in 1948 and were ordained by the German High Priest, Venerable Nyanatiloka Maha Thera of the Island Hermitage, Dodanduwa, Galle, Sri Lanka. [See *A Gist of Dhamma* for a brief account of their life and works.]

Venerable Nanavira Thera [Harold Musson], an Englishman, had graduated at the age of twenty-one from Cambridge with first class honors in modern languages. He was also a mathematician. After having made a deep study of the Canon and scriptures, and spending his time as a recluse in the Bundala dry zone forest, in southern Sri Lanka, while adhering to the traditions of the noble disciples [*aryasavaka*], he rejected everything which he regarded as not being the words of the Buddha, beginning with the Abhidhamma Pitaka. He therefore recommended the following books as the only trustworthy ones:

*Vinayapitaka: Suttavibhanga, Mahavagga, Culavagga, Suttapitaka Dighanikaya, Majjimanikaya, Samyuttanikaya, Anguttaranikaya, Suttanipata, Dhammapada, Udana, Itivuttaka, Theratherigatha.**

Venerable Nanamoli Thera [Osbert Moore] was from Oxford and was formerly the head of the Italian section of the BBC in London. His main works are the translations of the *Visuddhimagga* of Buddhagosa, [The Path of Purification] and the *Majjhima Nikaya*. Venerable Nanavira Thera wrote only one book, *Clearing the Path* and when published in

---

*The source material for this book is from this list.

1987, was reviewed in Europe as 'the most important book of the century'. [See Annexure]

The Dhamma was taught by the Buddha at two levels: mundane for the householder or the uninstructed commoner (*puthajjana*) and supramundane, for the recluses and disciples of the Buddha who had renounced the world and the intentions of the householder. There is an incident recorded when the Buddha's chief lay supporter Anathapindika was dying and Venerable Ananda visited him and spoke some words of the Dhamma at the deep end. Ananda asked if he was foundering. 'When this was said, the householder Anathapindika wept and shed tears'. He said that he wept because he had never heard such a talk on the Dhamma. Venerable Ananda replied, "Such talk on the Dhamma, householder, is not given to lay people clothed in white. Such talk on the Dhamma is given to those who have gone forth."

This book seeks to interpret briefly and precisely, all the essential concepts in the teaching of the Buddha, with guidance from the writings of Nanavira Thera. I have followed his advice to ignore the commentaries, as they are unreliable. Readers may find some parts difficult on a first reading. Remember that understanding the Dhamma departs, after a certain stage of linear, logical reasoning, from inferential knowledge to intuition and insight, referred in the Dhamma as 'seeing' or *nanadassana*. Note also that the teaching is subtle and *patisotagami* or 'against the stream' of conventional thinking.

The Buddha used words that were in popular usage. He did not invent words but he gave commonly used words new shades of meanings in the special context he used them. "Phrasing is a mere trifle," he said. It is the meaning that is relevant. "Here, *bhikkhus*, some misguided men learn the Dhamma—discourses, stanzas, expositions, verses, exclamations, sayings, birth stories, marvels, and answers to questions—but having learned the Dhamma, they do not examine the meaning of those teachings with wisdom. Not examining the meaning of those teachings with wisdom, they do not gain a reflective acceptance of them. Instead they learn the Dhamma only for the sake of criticising others and winning in debates, and they do not experience the good for the sake of which they learned the Dhamma. Those teachings, being wrongly grasped by them, conduce to their harm and suffering for a long time." [M 22.10]

In the usage of the Dhamma, words such as *sanna* [perception], *cetana* [intention], *sankhara* [determinations] have subtle meanings. There is much confusion in the correct understanding of the Dhamma sometimes because quarrelling about the meaning of words is an occupational disease of scholars and professors. Ignorance of etymology (and phonology) will not prevent path entry [to Nibbana] but attachment to words will certainly obstruct progress in the understanding and practice of the Dhamma.

When you study the Dhamma note to look for **two** outstanding features. First, notice that the Buddha is the greatest analyser of phenomena of all times. But unlike others of his time and afterwards, in philosophy, metaphysics or science, the Buddha does not *push the analysis* further than is relevant to the only 'problem' he set out to solve. The problem is *dukkha*. He repeatedly says, "Both formerly and now, bhikkhus, what I teach is *dukkha* and the cessation of *dukkha*". While walking in the Sinsapa forest, he picked up a fistful of leaves and told the bhikkhus, "This is what I have taught you. What I have **not** taught you is as the leaves in the forest. Why? Because those things are useless, not relevant, not beneficial.

Remember what I have declared as declared, and what I have not declared, as not declared. Do not waste time on things not relevant to the problem of *dukkha*." "There is nothing more harmful," he said, "than wrong view [*miccaditthi*]". "Just as the dawn heralds and foretells the rising of the sun, so right view [*sammaditthi*] heralds and foretells the penetration to the **four noble truths**[1] according as they are".

Secondly, in his analysis, the Buddha is not interested in the *particular*. He speaks of what is *general* or underlying. For example, the invariable nature of phenomena is that they are all conditioned. That is, they are things [*dhamma*] that are dependent on other things, and therefore, inherently unstable, subject to fading, change and impermanence. Things, upon which other things depend, in terms of the Dhamma, are determinations [*sankhara.*] To take another example, whatever the mind is inclined to think is necessarily conditioned by our primordial underlying tendencies, taints or defilements—lust [*lobha*], hatred [*dosa*], ignorance [*moha*] of the Dhamma. His teaching is about the innate *inclination* of the mind, of the general nature of the mind. As you study the Dhamma, with a grasp of these two features you will note that the Dhamma is a *description of the essence or the general nature of phenomena*.

The Dhamma is not an explanation of experience. In the Dhamma, the 'world' is the body and mind that experiences things in consciousness. There is nothing, you may agree, that can be said about the world apart from consciousness. Whatever we can say about the world is necessarily relative to ourself. The word 'absolute' has no meaning. All internal and external stimuli that contact [*phassa*] with consciousness [*vinnana*] produce instant *affect*. "I teach the Dhamma to the person who feels", says Buddha. "It is only *dukkha* that arises, and it is only *dukkha* that ceases". "Just as the ocean has only one taste, the taste of salt," he says, "this teaching has only one taste, the taste of liberation".

Buddhism is today regarded as 'the fastest spreading religion in the West'. The word 'Buddhism' was coined by the British to give a name to the beliefs, practices, rites, rituals, traditions, folk lore, texts, art, sculpture and archeological findings during their colonial period of South East Asia, chiefly in Burma, Sri Lanka and India, though it had more or less 'vanished' in the India of Queen Victoria. While there is Dhamma in Buddhism, *there is no Buddhism in Dhamma*. I shall use the word 'Dhamma' to refer to the Teaching of the Buddha and quote words of the Buddha from the texts to guarantee authenticity to this introductory presentation of the teaching of the Buddha.

Please note there is repetition in this collection of essays to enable you to read them from anywhere in the book. The theme is *anatta*.

Notes

1. The four noble truths [*Ariya-Sacca*] are stated thus:

    (i) The noble truth of suffering. 'Birth is suffering, aging is suffering, sickness is suffering, death is suffering; sorrow and lamentation, pain, grief and despair are suffering; association with the loathed is suffering, dissociation from the loved is suffering, not to get what wants is suffering; in short, the five aggregates affected by holding are suffering'. [S 56:11]

(ii)   The noble truth of the origin of suffering. 'It is craving, which renews being, and is accompanied by relish and lust, relishing this and that – in other words, craving for sensual desires, craving for being, craving for non-being. But whereon does this craving arise and flourish? Wherever there is that which seems lovable and gratifying, thereon it arises and flourishes'. [D 22]

(iii)   The noble truth of the cessation of suffering. 'It is the remainderless fading and cessation of that same craving, the rejecting, relinquishing, leaving and renouncing of it. But whereon is this craving abandoned and made to cease? Wherever there is that which seems lovable and gratifying, thereon it is abandoned and made to cease'. [D 22]

(iv)   The noble truth of the way leading to the cessation of suffering. 'It is this Noble Eightfold Path [*Ariyo atthangiko maggo*], that is to say: right view [*samma-ditthi*], right intention [*samma-sankappa*], right speech [*samma-vaca*], right action [*samma-kammanta*], right livelihood [*samma-ajiva*], right effort [*samma-vayama*], right mindfulness [*samma-sati*], and right concentration [*samma-samadhi*]'. [D 22]

Chapter Two

The Birth and Passing Away
of the Buddha

Recent dating places the Buddha contemporaneous with Sophocles, the Greek playwright and tragedian [496-406 BC]. Other sages of these times are Socrates, Lao-tse, Confucius and Mahavira. 'Indian history actually begins with the story of the Buddha Gotama's life: or to put it perhaps more exactly, that is the point where history as record replaces archaeology and legend; for the documents of the Buddha's life and teaching—the earliest Indian documents to be accorded historical standing—reveal a civilization already stable and highly developed which can only have matured after a very long period indeed'[1]. He was born as Siddharata Gotama, the son of king Suddhodana and queen Mahamaya of a small tribal state, at Kapilavatthu, in the Nepal border of India, in the foothills of the Himalayas.

The renunciation of the Buddha is recorded in the *Pitakas*[2] in 'striking bare simplicity'. 'Later, while still young, a black-haired boy blessed with youth, in the first phase of life, I shaved off my hair and beard—though my mother and father wished otherwise and grieved with tearful faces—and I put on the yellow robe and went forth from the house life into homelessness'.[3] His mother Mahamaya had died seven days after he was born on a full moon day in May, and he was brought up by her sister Mahapajapati. When he left home, Siddharata was twenty-nine years old and it is said that on that day his son Rahula was born to his wife Yasodhara. 'Rahula' was thus named, meaning 'a bond'. The boy was later to become a disciple under him when the latter returned home for the first time as the Buddha, about nine years later.

The struggle to attain Enlightenment [Samma-sambodhi] lasted six years of enormous striving and self-denial, as was the tradition of those times in the way to spiritual advancement. Though literature of a later date supplies many details of the early years, the Tipitaka itself has very little to say about them. There is, in fact, only reference to two incidents: firstly, the reminiscence of the meditation under the rose-apple tree while the Bodhisatta's[4] father was working—doing the ceremonial ploughing at the opening of the sowing season, as the Commentary[5] says, and secondly, there is the account of the 'three considerations,' which correspond to three 'messengers' [the old, the sick and the dead]. On the first occasion, he was perhaps about five years old and on the second, in the early 20s, before marriage, skilled in learning and sports as would befit an heir to the throne.

Tradition is that though seers summoned to 'examine' the new-born Siddharata predicted the renunciation, and though his father took extraordinary measures to prevent exposing his son to ordinary secular life, Siddharata experienced insight into old age, decay and death on three separate occasions when outside the guarded premises of his three palaces.

The Buddha says, "When I considered [this], the vanity of youth, the vanity of health and the vanity of life entirely left me".

He led the holy life under two of the foremost masters of *samadhi* meditation[6] and he says, " … entered upon and dwelt in this teaching, myself realising it through direct knowledge". However they both placed him as their equal. He continued saying, "I thought: 'This teaching does not lead to dispassion, to fading of lust, to cessation, to peace, to direct knowledge, to enlightenment, to Nibbana[7] but to the base of nothingness …to the base of neither-perception-nor-non-perception[8]. I was not satisfied with that teaching. I left to pursue my search." And he continues thus, " … I wandered by stages through the Magadhan country and at length arrived at Senanigama near Uruvela[9]. There I saw an agreeable plot of ground, a delightful grove, a clear-flowing river with pleasant smooth banks, and nearby a village as alms resort. I thought: 'This will serve for the struggle of a clansman who seeks the struggle'." There he sat at the root of a banyan tree determined never to get up till he was convinced he found what he was searching.

Earlier, while studying under the two masters of *samadhi* meditation with five other pupils, the memory when as a child he sat under a rose-apple tree came to him and he had attained the first *jhana*[10]. He says, "I thought: 'Might this be the way to enlightenment … Why am I afraid of pleasure? It is pleasure that has nothing to do with *sensual* desires and unwholesome things …' It is not possible to attain that pleasure with a body so excessively emaciated. Suppose I ate some solid food – some boiled rice and bread. Now at that time, five bhikkhus[11] were waiting upon me thinking, 'If the monk Gotama achieves something, he will tell us … ' As soon as I ate the solid food, the boiled rice and bread, the five bhikkhus were disgusted and left me, thinking: 'The monk Gotama has become indulgent, he has given up the struggle and has reverted to luxury'."

The enlightenment of the Buddha is described in several Suttas or discourses: "I entered upon and abode in the first meditation, which is accompanied by thinking and exploring, with happiness and pleasure born of seclusion. But I allowed no such pleasant feeling as arose in me to gain power over my mind. With the stilling of thinking and exploring I entered upon and abode in the second meditation, which has internal confidence and singleness of mind without thinking and exploring, with happiness and pleasure born of concentration. But I allowed no such pleasant feeling as arose in me to gain power over my mind. With the fading as well of happiness, I abode in equanimity, mindful and fully aware; still feeling pleasure with the body, I entered upon and abode in the third meditation, referring to which the noble ones announce: 'He has a pleasant abiding who looks on with equanimity and is mindful'. But I allowed no such ... over my mind."

In this way, he reached a ninth meditative state, one higher than his former two teachers, breaking through the barrier of thinking, of conceiving, to the base of 'neither feeling nor perception'. "When my concentrated mind was thus purified ... I directed, inclined my mind to the knowledge of recollection of past lives. I recollected my manifold past lives ... this was *the first true knowledge attained by me in the first watch of the night* ... When my concentrated mind was thus purified ... I saw beings passing away and reappearing, inferior and superior, fair and ugly, happy and unhappy in their destinations... I understood how beings pass on according to their actions. This *was the second true knowledge attained by me in the second watch of the night…* When my concentrated mind was thus purified … I directed, I inclined my mind to the knowledge of exhaustion of taints[12]. I had direct knowledge, as it actually is, that *'This is suffering'*, that *'This is the origin of suffering'*, that *'This is the cessation of suffering …, 'This is the way leading to the cessation of taints'*. Knowing thus and seeing thus my heart was liberated from the taint of sensual desire, from the taint of being, and from the taint of ignorance. When liberated … there came the knowledge … birth is exhausted, the holy life has been lived out, what was to be done is done, there is no more of this to come'. This *was the third true knowledge attained by me in the third watch of the night".*

Siddharata Gotama had attained Enlightenment, become the 'Awakened One', attained the unformed, the undetermined Nibbana at the age of thirty-five. He lived for forty-five years more, walking perhaps 50,000 miles, teaching the Dhamma he directly saw and understood, after initial hesitation. He told a brahmin who met him years later, as to many others, "This Dhamma, Vaccha, is profound, hard to see and hard to understand, peaceful and sublime, unattainable mere reasoning, subtle, to be experienced by the wise."

The Buddha gradually established a monastic order of disciples—of bhikkhus and bhikkhunis—known collectively as the Sangha, inviting any person who desired to learn from him and abide in a solemn verbal agreement of the rules of discipline [*Vinaya*] he made as the occasion or individual behaviour indicated to him. He was hesitant to ordain women but was persuaded by Ananda to admit his foster mother Mahapajapati Gotama at her request, as the first bhikkhuni, which order, thereafter, flourished for some time. Usually, there was a 3-4 months period of probation before conformation in the 'higher ordination'. Admission to the Sangha was done by the Buddha or by authorised senior disciples. "Lord, we wish to receive the going forth and the full admission from the Blessed One." "Come, bhikkhus," the Blessed One said, "the Dhamma is well proclaimed; lead the holy life for the complete ending of suffering." It was simple and straightforward – no rites, no ceremony. The last person to be ordained in his epic life was 'the wanderer Subhadda', a few minutes before he passed away ignoring the protestation of Ananda, who was screening the large gathering of former relatives and clansmen who had come to pay their respects.

On many occasions, the texts refer to hundreds of bhikkhus gathering in halls or in outdoor parks to listen to the Buddha. He had tremendous charisma, as several have commented on meeting him, sometimes to learn, or intending to defeat him in debate. The most outstanding noted by various kings, and admired even by rival teachers was the absolute *silence* that prevailed when the Buddha was teaching. He had a clear, pleasant voice. He placed great stress on proper attention [*yoniso manasikara*] as a necessary tenet of the Dhamma for progress in spiritual advancement.

He had farsight. "Bhikkhus, be my heirs in Dhamma, not my heirs in material things," said he to discourage icons and worship [M 3.2]. He was utterly consistent and profound whenever he spoke. He never indulged in gossip. And he never issued commandments. He is the only teacher to invite investigation of his teachings and reflective acceptance. Four kinds of expressions used by the Buddha, as mentioned by him, are:

1. Telling the seen as it is seen.
2. Telling the heard as it is heard.

3. Telling the sensed as it is sensed.

4. Telling the cognised as it is cognised[13] [MN 112.3].

The Buddha took only one meal a day – in the forenoon – and slept, it is said, only for two hours a day, mentally noting the time to rise. "Bhikkhus, I eat at a single session. By so doing, I am free from illness and affliction, and I enjoy health, strength and a comfortable abiding" [M 21.7]. He always led by example and was democratic in taking decisions and teaching. "Speak only of what you have known, seen and understood for yourself," he often advised. "I do not see even a single kind of form, Ananda, from the change and alteration of which there would not arise sorrow, lamentation, pain, grief and despair *in one who lusts for it and takes delight in it.*" "The effort you must yourself make. The Perfect Ones point the way" [Dhp 276]. "Thus I speak of the abandoning even of the base of neither-perception-nor-non-perception. Do you see Udayin, any fetter[14], small or great of whose abandoning I do not speak?" [M 66.34]. He was a great 'physician'. "If you want to get well, you must yourself take the treatment prescribed. You shall not get well if instead you just admire the medicine and the physician."

The Buddha stands out as a teacher *par excellence* in the use of simile, metaphor and satire. There are enough similes in the Dhamma for a compendium. Describing hindrances[15] [*nivarana*] that prevent mental development and *samadhi*, he used the simile of water [See notes]. The lotus was his favourite. He was able to adapt the most humdrum object to help understanding and insight into the core teaching. "Bhikkhus, what do you think? If people carried off the grass, sticks, branches, and leaves in this Jeta Grove, or burned them, or did what they liked with them, would you think: 'People are carrying us off or burning us or doing what they like with us?' "No, Venerable sir". "Why not?" "Because that is neither our self nor what belongs to our self." "So too, bhikkhus, whatever is not yours, abandon it. What is it that is not yours? Material form [*rupa*] is not yours ... Feeling [*vedana*] is not yours ... Perception [*sanna*] is not yours ... Determinations [*sankhara*] are not yours ... Consciousness [*vinnana*] is not yours. Abandon it. When you have abandoned it, that will lead to your welfare and happiness for a long time" [M 22.41].

Here is a more recondite example. "Just as a flame blown by the wind's force, Upasiva," said the Blessed One, "goes out and designation applies to it no more, so too the Silent Sage, being freed from the name-body goes out, and designation applies to him no more ... There is no measuring of one who has gone out, Upasiva, and nothing of him whereby one could say ought of him; for when all ideas have been abolished, all ways of saying too have been abolished"[16]. Thus, the Buddha often referred to himself as the Tathagatha, the 'one thus gone'.

The Buddha did not act as if he was divine. He was a unique human teacher. For example, he did not hesitate to reprimand. "Misguided man," he told bhikkhu Arittha, "to whom have you ever known me to teach the Dhamma in that way?" He was probably the first person in the world to establish 'relevance' as a determining principle in the technology of teaching and in interactive education. "What do you think, Rahula?" asked the Buddha from his young son. "What is the purpose of a mirror?" "For the purpose of reflection, Venerable sir". "So too, Rahula, an action with the body should be done after repeated reflection; an action by speech should be done after repeated reflection; an action by mind should be done after repeated reflection ... never tell a lie even as a joke!"

He used repetition as a principle of his teaching technique. There was humour and satire in some of his exchanges with haughty brahmins. 'Once, the wanderer Dighanakha said, "Master Gotama, my doctrine and view is this: 'Nothing is acceptable to me'." The Buddha asked, "This view of yours, 'Nothing is acceptable to me' – is not at least that view acceptable to you?" [M 74.1]

When you read the Suttas, you will notice that the Buddha strings his words with incomparable simplicity, orderliness, and completes the sentence so that not one word can be missed out or misplaced without altering its meaning. He had a remarkable ability to instantly enumerate complicated concepts as for example, saying, "The eighteen kinds of mental exploration should be understood." [M 137.8]. He often gave a synopsis of his discourse at the beginning, repeated things in different ways and presented the Dhamma structured and tailored to each occasion. So, it is not said with exaggeration that if anyone has spoken perfectly, it is the Buddha.

Prominent brahmins and contemporary teachers, ascetics such as Nigantha Nataputta [Mahavira] commonly addressed the Buddha, in his time, as 'Master Gotama'. He was for some elliptic reason known as *muni*, the Silent Sage. The 'silence' of the Buddha is a deep subject for interpretation. Silence was perhaps the best of his teaching skills. He used four methods to answer questions put to him. Briefly, he would answer with a short 'yes' or 'no' or he would give a detailed discourse; or he would question in turn to let the questioner arrive at the answer himself; and, he was silent when the question did not arise. The well-known event is with Vacchagotta. On one occasion the wanderer Vacchagotta went to the Blessed One and exchanged greetings with him. Then he asked, "How is it, Master Gotama, does self exist?" When this was said, the Blessed One was silent. "How is it, then, Master Gotama, does self not exist?" And for a second time the Blessed One was silent. Then Vacchagotta got up from his seat and went away [S 44.10]. This episode is sometimes misunderstood to mean that the Buddha prevaricated on the question of 'self'. The Buddha rightly did not respond. *To answer a question is to accept that it can be asked.* The Buddha was also silent when he was invited for a meal, indicating thereby that he accepted the invitation.

The Buddha went into short periods of meditative retreat to take a break from his arduous ministry and recuperate from brief episodes of sickness. Throughout his ministry, he took care of his physical health. Venerable Jivaka was his personal physician. He suffered from food poisoning probably from a meal served from truffles, a few weeks before passing away. The *parinibbana* of the Buddha, at Kusinara, by the roadside, under a *Sal* tree said to have blossomed out of season, near his hometown, is described in haunting prose by his cousin Venerable Ananda who was his personal attendant for the last twenty-five years. "Now I am old, Ananda, my years have turned eighty: just as an old cart is made to carry on with the help of makeshifts, so too, it seems to me, the Perfect One's body is made to carry on with the help of makeshifts ... Therefore, Ananda, each of you should make himself his island, himself and no other his refuge; each of you should make the Dhamma his island, the Dhamma and no other his refuge."

Before leaving on his last journey he said, "Ananda, go and summon all the bhikkhus in the neighborhood of Vesali to meet in the service hall". When assembled, he spoke thus: "Bhikkhus, I have now taught you things that I have directly known; these things you should learn thoroughly and maintain in being, develop and constantly put into effect so that this holy life may endure long. You should do so for the welfare and happiness of gods and men. And what are these things? They are the four stations of mindfulness, the four right endeavours, the four bases for success, the five spiritual faculties, the five spiritual powers, the seven enlightenment factors, and the Noble Eightfold Path. I have taught you these things, having directly known them. These[17] you should thoroughly learn ... for the good and welfare and happiness of gods and men ... Indeed, bhikkhus, I declare this to you: It is in the nature of all determinations to dissolve. Attain perfection through diligence. Soon the Blessed One will attain final Nibbana." And in immortal last words he reiterated, a few minutes before passing away: "It is in the nature of all determinations to dissolve. Attain perfection through diligence. [*Vayadhamma sankhara. Appamadena sampadetha.*]" With these four words, the Buddha summarised his forty-five years of teaching. [*Mahaparinibbana Sutta*]

Notes

1. Bhikkhu Nanamoli, *The Life of the Buddha*, Buddhist Publication Society, Kandy, Sri Lanka, 3rd ed. 1992, p.1.

2. *Tipitaka* or the Pali Canon are the *Sutta-Pitaka* [Discourses], *Vinaya-Pitaka* [Rules of monastic discipline], *Abhidhamma-Pitaka* [Higher Dhamma].

3. M. 26, 36, 85, 100.

4. The term describes the Buddha in previous lives and before Enlightenment.

5. The traditional Commentaries of the Dhamma.

6. Samadhi [concentration] or serenity through meditation was well-known and widely practiced during and before the time of the Buddha. The Buddha additionally taught *Vipassana* [Insight] meditation and recommended developing both 'yoked together'.

7. Nibbana means 'extinction'. There are 33 words or terms such as The Non-Determined [*Asankhata*], The Beyond [*Param*], The Not-decaying [*Ajaram*]. The Subtle [*Nipunam*], The Non-Indicative [*Anidassanam*] used to denote the 'state of final liberation' [*Vimutti*] or 'end of *dukkha*'. It is cessation of feeling and perception.

8. Under his first teacher, Siddharata achieved the base consisting of nothingness and thereafter under his second teacher, achieved the higher base consisting of neither-perception-nor-non-perception in the immaterial meditative or *arupa* absorption or states.

9. Located near modern Benaras.

10. The *jhanas* are mundane meditative states consisting of four stages of meditative experience. The first *jhana* is accompanied by applied and sustained thinking pervaded by rapture and pleasure born of seclusion, the second by singleness of mind pervaded by rapture and pleasure born of concentration, the third is pervaded by pleasure 'divested' of rapture and in the 4th and last material *jhana*, there is experience of purity of mind due to equanimity [*upekkha*] when breathing stops.

11. The five friends who studied along with him under the masters Vappa, Bhaddiya, Mahanama, Assaji, Kondanna. The last named was one of 8 seers who had 'examined' the new-born Siddharata, and he was the first *arahat* after the Buddha, to penetrate the Dhamma when the Buddha taught his very first discourse, the *Dhammacakka-pavattana-sutta* [Setting Rolling the Wheel of the Dhamma] to them.

12. The taints or *kilesa* or primordial mental defilements are: the taint of sensual desire, the taint of desire for being, the taint of ignorance or of views [M 2].

13. This is a cryptic statement that goes to the root of Dhamma. It means that he speaks of 'things as they actually are' [*yathabhuta*], that is, without things being regarded as pointing to a subject because in truth [*saccato thetato*], there is no 'self' or 'me' or 'I'. The 'self' is a mental construction, a delusion of a delusion, arising from ignorance of Dhamma [avijja].

14. The 10 fetters [*samyojana*] that enslave persons to being [*bhava*] or re-becoming are listed as lower and higher. The lower fetters are: (i) The personality view [*sakkaya-ditthi*]. (ii) Uncertainty [*vicikiccha*]. (iii) Misapprehension virtue and duty/adherence to rites, rules and regulations [*silabbata-paramasa*]. (iv) Sensuous craving [*kama-raga*]. (v) Ill-will [*vyapada*]. The higher are: (i) Craving for fine-material existence [*rupa-raga*]. (ii) Craving for immaterial existence [*arupa-raga*]. (iii) Conceit [*mana*]. (iv) Restlessness [*uddhacca*], and (v) Ignorance of the four noble truths [*Avijja*]. They are abandoned gradually ending in becoming *arahat* when all *samyojana* are extirpated. He who is free from 1-3

is a stream-winner or *sotapanna*, ie one who has entered the stream
to Nibbana. He who additionally overcomes 4 and 5 in their gross
form is a Once-returner or *sakadagami*. He who is fully free from
1-5 is an *Anagami* or Non-returner attaining Nibbana from the
Pure Abodes. He that is free from all 10 is the *arahat* ie a perfectly
Holy One like the Buddha.

15. The five hindrances [*nivarana*] are imperfections of the mind that
weaken wisdom [M 112.18]. They are: (i) Sensuality
[*kamacchanda*] – compared to multicoloured water (ii) Ill-will
[*vayapada*] – compared to boiling water. (iii) Lethargy and
drowsiness [*thinna-middha*] – compared to water covered with
moss. (iv) Agitation and worry [*Uddhacca-kukkucca*] – compared
to water whipped by wind. (v) Doubt or uncertainty [*Vicikiccha*]
– compared to turbid and muddy water.

16. This simile is used to describe that the *arahat* has finally extirpated
the conceit 'I' and 'mine' and cannot be said to exist as a 'person'.
The *arahat* is an 'individual', a discrete unit of consciousness and
matter. "This body is not yours, nor another's but is past action
[already] determined and chosen that must be experienced to be
seen." Thus, the *arahat* is not described in terms of 'birth' and
'death'. The *arahat* has 'attained Nibbana here and now'. "Friend,
when this body is bereft of three states—vitality, heat and
consciousness – it is discarded and forsaken, left lying senseless
like a log" [M 43.24]. Limitation of language demands use of
words such as 'he' and 'me' without misapprehension.

17. *Bodhipakkhiyadhamma* [37 items - The Ascesis of Awakening]

Chapter Three

Logic and Reasoning in the Dhamma

The great attractiveness of the teachings of the Buddha in the West among intellectuals and thinking young people that we see today is largely due to the underlying reason and logic of the Dhamma. In more than seven thousand discourses of the Buddha extant today, nowhere has he issued commandments or stated an arrogant opinion or dogma to be accepted willy-nilly without question. The discourses are replete with appeal to rational and clear thinking inviting anyone to investigate and scrutinise them, and gain a reflective acceptance of the teaching.

The theme that runs throughout the teaching and upon which it is based is: *Not, this is mine; not, this am I; not, this is my self.* The greatest difficulty in the Dhamma lies here in penetrating the meaning of those few words that anchor the entire teaching to the aim of liberation here and now, in this very life, not after death in some remote future.

The first and immediate problem is that the statement goes against the grain of universal conventional feeling and thinking of a discrete 'personality' we each possess from birth, which everyone sets out to develop and maintain till death. The second difficulty is the limitation imposed by language to continue to use words such as 'I' and 'me' and 'mine' and 'you' in any discussion of 'personality'. The Buddha was eminently aware of them and he tackled both in a variety of ways using logic and reasoning to open our minds to a true understanding and penetration that there is in fact no one here.

The methods he used to guide the earnest student of the Dhamma from inferential thinking to insight are however subtle. Throughout the teaching, the exhortation he makes is this: *Accept only when in you 'this is true'.* Let me now give in outline some of the teaching methods used by the Buddha in regard to 'self'.

1. It is not by reasoning that we naturally come to regard, 'This is mine, this am I, this is my self'. The concept of a person, a self comes about *affectively*. The outstanding evidence of being is that we feel. From the moment of birth, feelings invade the consciousness and remain even fleetingly as evocations of sights, sounds, smell, tastes, touches and ideas. They rise and fall. Feelings tether us to self. And this, the Dhamma says, is the existential problem. The arising and cessation of feeling, the Buddha taught, is necessarily dependent on three things and their contact with consciousness or the mind. For example, the three things, the fleshy eye and its internal base, external percepts of form or shape or colour, and eye-consciousness react together instantly when they make contact with the mind, the fundamental feature of which is that contact is with 'me'. There now arises feelings dependent on the eye. Thus we say, 'I like' or 'I dislike' or 'I neither like nor

dislike what I see'. But why it cannot be said, 'There is liking ... nor disliking' without reference to a person? Why cannot feeling be mere feeling without being labelled 'my feeling' or 'your feeling'? If in truth there were no 'person' or 'self' that is contacted by the confluence of the three things—eye, forms, eye-consciousness— would the benefit of the outcome be tremendous? Would there be neither sorrow nor joy? Would there be dispassion and not passion? All personal and inter-personal conflicts that arise within our experience from feeling in the seen shall now not arise because reflection would tell that feeling is feeling brought about by mere contact [*phassa*] and not by contact with a person that feels. The Buddha generalises, 'This world is tormented by contact [with self]'. When the 'self' is abandoned and not clung-to, there is peace. There is now no torment or agitation or reaction in the seen, the heard, the sensed and the cognised. There is insight of things as they actually are. In the seen is merely the seen, in the heard merely the heard, in the sensed merely the sensed and in the cognised merely the cognised.

2. This body of ours is continually disintegrating. The parts and the total of them are relentlessly breaking down from the moment of birth till death. No single thing or the millions of processes that make this body a living monolithic whole is free from affliction. No feeling or perception or intention that arise from contact with 'me' lasts for ever. There can be no dispute about this characteristic of impermanence. So long there exists 'me', the feeling of impermanence is *subjective*. So long as we appropriate experiences by the five senses and the mind, and put mental constructions or

intentions upon them, so long there is disappointment, dissatisfaction, suffering, sorrow or *dukkha*. It follows therefore that disappointment, dissatisfaction, suffering, sorrow or *dukkha* arises because there is craving to hold to fleeting, fading, changing, impermanent feelings [and other things] which stem from ignorance because in actual fact there is no one here that feels or exists. It follows that there is escape from all feelings when the holding to a belief in 'me or self that feels' is abandoned. That is what the Buddha teaches. How to escape is what he teaches us to practise. How to escape is more than mere reasoning, logic and intellectual acceptance of the deception of a 'self'. Reasoning, thinking and pondering leads to escape or liberation from dukkha if the instructions of the Buddha in this regard are rigorously practised. He gives firm assurance from his own experience and additionally tells us, *'There is no reason why I should want to deceive you.'*

3. Is feeling monitored by self? While feelings change, fade and disappear, is there an unchanging permanent self that monitors feeling? Feelings can be pleasant, unpleasant or neutral. Feelings arise from the data streaming in from the five senses and the mind. Since all three feelings are not present at one and the same time, and if feeling is self, should there not be three different selves, one at each time? If self on the other hand is not feeling but some independent entity, and if it is this unchanging permanent self that receives and monitors feelings, should this self not have *mastery* over these feelings [and over other things]? Should this self not be able to command: 'Let me have this feeling, let me not have this

feeling?' But if it actually is not the case that there is such a master, would holding to a belief in a master that is undermined by change, fading and impermanence not be a mockery? Reasoning and logic when thus applied to all feelings that are necessarily impermanent, on reflection, leads to acceptance that holding to a belief in an unchanging permanent self is not rational.

The above three instances of reasoning applied in the Dhamma are given as a sample albeit in outline. There is more in many of the discourses that is outside the scope of this essay. The Buddha is the only teacher to frankly invite scrutiny of his teaching. He presented himself as a teacher who merely points the way. And he says, before you examine his teaching, [or anything else], it is wise to begin with at least provisional faith in the teacher. No blind faith thereafter is required. Intelligent study and examination of the meaning of the Dhamma rationally without bias or pre-determined views lead to wisdom and insight of which there is no doubt. That is the method and style of the Dhamma.

Chapter Four

The Buddha's Concept of Dukkha

Fundamental Structure

The Buddha did not discover dukkha. Everyone before and in his time knew there is dukkha in existence. What he discovered was the *structure* of the arising and cessation of dukkha. He realised that whenever a 'thing' is dependent on some 'other thing' and when this 'other thing' is impermanent, the 'thing' upon which the 'other thing' depends too is impermanent; and whatever is impermanent is dukkha. This is the fundamental structure of dependent origination of existence or being, of birth, decay, death and dukkha. 'When this is this is. When this arises this arises. When this is not this is not. When this ceases this ceases'[1]. If so, upon what precisely is this 'thing' dukkha dependent? The teachings of the Buddha for forty-five years is the answer to this question.

Definition of Dukkha

In the Dhamma, dukkha is defined in a variety of ways. The conventional and easily understood definition is that dukkha is sorrow and lamentation, pain, grief and despair, separation from loved ones, from associating with those whom one does not like and from not getting what one wants. After describing this worldly concept of dukkha, the Buddha made a quantum leap and declared, "In short, the five aggregates of form, feeling, perception, determinations and consciousness affected by holding [*upadana*] are dukkha." No one before the Buddha, in this epoch, had made the stunning statement that this body in fact is dukkha. Since dukkha is feeling, and since there must be a person that feels, it follows that so long as there is a person who thinks 'this body is mine or it belongs to me', there shall always be dukkha. In other words, dukkha depends on the persistence of the primordial ignorance that this body is not 'mine'.

Spectrum of Dukkha

The word 'dukkha' cannot be expressed in any other one word to capture the full spectrum of its meaning as taught by the Buddha. In addition to sorrow, lamentation, pain, grief, despair, it describes dissatisfaction, discontent, frustration, disappointment, unfulfilment and suffering. It refers to conflicts that arise within ourselves and with others from adherence to feelings, perceptions, intentions, conceit, ideas, views and opinions of ourselves and of the world around us. It refers to problems, disputes, jealousy, covetousness and all unprofitable things that originate from in-born tendencies to like and dislike, from inclinations to cling, want and appropriate. It refers to the danger of attaching ourselves to sensual desires that change, fade and do not last. "I do not see a single form, Ananda, from the change and alteration of which there shall not arise dukkha in one who desires and lusts for it," says the Buddha.

Nature of Dukkha

Dhamma is about the nature of this body [including mind] and its interaction with the world around it—and with nothing else. It is wrong to extrapolate it to things such as politics, psychology, science, evolution and so on. While discussion of the Dhamma with other things is interesting, it is a waste of time. Time is the very essence of existence. We have wasted millions of years in ignorance, by not awakening to the arising of dukkha and the way to escape from it, by not hearing the Dhamma and practising it and that it is foolish to waste time any further, when given the opportunity once in the life-stream. The Buddha thus frequently tells his disciples, "Both formerly and now, what I teach and describe is dukkha and the cessation of dukkha ...Virtue, learning, discussion, serenity and insight lead to right view and penetration of the Dhamma ... Meditate. Do not delay or you will regret later." Finally, a few minutes before he passed away he repeated what he had also said on many occasions, "It is the nature of determinations to disappear. Strive with diligence." [*Vayadhamma sankhara, appamadena sampadetha.*]

Unique View of Dukkha

We can now take a look at dukkha in the precise unique way of the Buddha. The *key word* is 'determinations' or *sankhara* in Pali. That is why he chose it to phrase his last words. Determinations are one of the five aggregates affected by holding [*upadana*]. The five aggregates [*khanda*] themselves are not dukkha. There is dukkha only when they are affected by holding. The result is dukkha. The feeling of dukkha arises only when we are attached to them and delight in the *khanda*. Why is that? Why is delight and holding to this body dukkha? The answer is far from obvious. In fact it seems preposterous that delight or pleasure or desire is dukkha. The secret of the Dhamma is in this riddle. Its core effort to understand is to unravel it. In a periodic statement the Buddha says, "All things have desire for their root, attention provides their being, contact their origin, feeling their meeting place, concentration the confrontation with them, mindfulness their control while, understanding is the highest of them and deliverance is their core."

Determinations of Dukkha

Let us now understand *sankhara*, one of the *khanda*, conjoined in consciousness with feeling and perception. Determinations are things upon which other things depend. Thus, feelings depend on contact [*phassa*]. Contact depends on the five senses. The five senses depend on consciousness. Birth depends on holding to the desire for being. Aging and death depends on birth. In this fundamental structure of dependent arising [and cessation], for example, 'contact' as we have seen is the determination or necessary condition for what it determines, namely feeling. In other words, determinations determine the determined, and determinations are themselves determined by other determinations. Determinations are bound with what they determine. They are not what they determine. As the Buddha says, "Determinations determine the determined. That is why they are called determinations."

Negativity of Determinations

The question can now be asked, "Are there determinations that do not determine anything?" The answer is that there cannot be because determinations must determine something. Furthermore, determinations are *negative*. They deny the existence of the positive as when the determination 'altruism' denies the existence of 'selfishness'. But while a determination is negative, it immediately asserts the existence of and essence of the positive. Altruism implies selfishness. When we know what 'altruism' means, we shall know what 'selfishness' means. When we come to understand dukkha, we shall arrive at experiencing bliss. Since feelings are bound to this body and this body and feelings are impermanent, we shall experience why what is impermanent is dukkha.

Impermanence of Determinations

The Buddha says, "This world is unstable." When we understand why what is dependent on some other thing is unstable, we shall understand why what is unstable is dukkha. When we understand that this body is unstable and impermanent, we shall understand that it is foolish to be attached to the body from regarding it as belonging to me. Our vicissitudes, our likes and dislikes, our natural ingrained habit of making inferences from this body, arise from determinations or intentions of one sort or another. Thus, the Buddha says, whatever is volitional is dukkha. It is the gist of the insight of dukkha. This is the unique description of dukkha by the Buddha: *"All determinations are impermanent. All determinations are dukkha."*

Notes

1. The statement is commonly translated wrong. 'When this is, that is.' In this form 'that' would mean any number of things. The word 'this' indicates specifically 'this'. Only Nanavira Thera makes the correct translation.

Chapter Five
The Story of Ratthapala

I have condensed this Sutta [M 82] to give a sample portrait of people who lived at the time of the Buddha and illustrate with a beautiful story how even the wealthiest were charmed by his teaching. It also describes the Dhamma at a mundane and higher level for reflection.

Once, the Buddha visited a certain town and when the people heard about it, they flocked to listen him teach. A young man, the only son of a very rich brahmin, went along with them. After the sermon, he approached the Buddha and said he wished to join the order. The Buddha asked him to first get the permission of his parents. Ratthapala went home and begged permission from his parents thus: "Mother and father, as I understand the Dhamma taught by the Blessed One, it is not easy while living in a home to lead the holy life, utterly perfect and pure as a polished shell. I wish to shave off my hair and beard, put on the yellow robe, and go forth from the home life into homelessness. Give me permission to go forth from the home life into homelessness".

The parents refused him three times. "Dear Ratthapala, you are our only son, dear and beloved. You have been raised in comfort, brought up in comfort; you know nothing of suffering, dear Ratthapala. Even in case of your death we would lose you unwillingly, so how could we give you permission to go forth from the home life into homelessness?" Then, Ratthapala lay down there on the bare floor, saying, "Right here I shall either die or receive the going forth". His parents called on his friends to advise Ratthapala and they too having failed, advised the parents to give permission saying that he might want to return if he does not enjoy the holy life. The father then gave him permission on condition he must visit his parents. Ratthapala immediately met the Buddha. Seeing the intensity of his faith in the Dhamma, he gave him full admission to the holy life.

Before long, by dwelling alone, keeping himself withdrawn, diligent, ardent and resolute, the Venerable Ratthapala with direct knowledge, realised for himself that supreme goal for the sake of which clansmen rightly go forth from home life into homelessness. He directly knew, "Birth is destroyed, the holy life has been lived, what had to be done has been done, there is no more coming to any state of being." And the Venerable Ratthapala became one of the *arahats*.

Years later, he asked the Buddha if he could visit his parents. Knowing that Ratthapala was 'incapable of abandoning the training and returning to the low life', the Buddha gave permission. At his hometown, the Venerable Ratthapala went for alms from house to house. Now on that occasion his father was sitting in the hall having his hair dressed when he saw a figure of a bhikkhu coming to his house. The man was enraged, and fumed, "Our only son was made to go forth by these bald-pated recluses!" and he chased the Venerable Ratthapala away. Just then a slave woman of one of his relatives was about to throw away some old porridge. Seeing this the Venerable Ratthapala said to her, "Sister, if that stuff is to be thrown away, then pour it into my bowl here". The woman recognised the characteristic features of his hands, his feet, and his voice. She ran and told his parents. The father rushed out. He saw the Venerable Ratthapala seated by a wall on the roadside, eating the stale porridge. He was very upset and invited him home. "Enough, householder, my meal for today is finished," said the Venerable Ratthapala. "Then, dear Ratthapala, consent to accept tomorrow's meal," said the father.

The Venerable Ratthapala accepted in silence and arrived home the next day from a royal park where he spent the night in meditation. Meanwhile, the father had gold coins and bullion made into a large heap and covered it with mats. Then he told Venerable Ratthapala's former wives to bedeck themselves with jewellery and perfume and lure his son back. And when the Venerable Ratthapala arrived in the morning, his father had the gold and bullion uncovered and said, "Dear Ratthapala, this is your maternal fortune; your paternal fortune is another and your ancestral fortune is another … ". He entreated him to revert to his former life at home and enjoy the wealth with his wives. The Venerable Ratthapala gently asked his father to load the gold and bullion into carts and dump the lot in the Ganges! "Why is that?" he asked. "Because, householder, on account of this there will arise for you sorrow, lamentation, pain, grief and despair." Then his former wives inquired, "What are they like, my lord's son, the nymphs for whose sake you lead the holy life?" "We do not lead the holy life for the sake of nymphs, sisters," said the Venerable Ratthapala. The women were aghast to be addressed as 'sister'. More entreaties were made. Finally, the Venerable Ratthapala told his father to either give him a meal if there was one prepared and requested not to cause him further harassment.

After the meal, he returned to the park to spend the day and night in meditation. The king in the area had by now come to hear of the return of the now famous renouncer and went to the park to meet him. "Master Ratthapala, there are four kinds of loss because [of which] … some go into homelessness. They are: loss through aging, loss through sickness, loss of wealth and loss of relatives," sermonised the king. He then expanded on these four kinds of loss and inquired which of the four made the Venerable Ratthapala leave home for the holy life? The detailed answers Venerable Ratthapala gave should be read in the Sutta. The king was so impressed that he entreated the Venerable Ratthapala to teach him some of the Dhamma of the Buddha. The teaching of the Venerable Ratthapala is a classic of summary. "Great king, there are four summaries of the Dhamma that has been taught by the Blessed One …

1. Any world is unstable, it is swept away.

2. Any world has no shelter and no protector.

3. Any world has nothing of its own; one has to leave all and pass away.

4. Any world is incomplete, insatiate, the slave of craving."

The Venerable Ratthapala then explained them to the king in a way he could relate to his own life in the following way [condensed]:

1. "Great king, were you, when young, strong, an expert in sports such as horsemanship, archery? Now are you strong in thighs, in arms and sturdy as before?" "No sir, I am burdened with years," said the king and continued, Sometimes I mean to put a foot here

and I put it somewhere else". Ratthapala answered, "It was on account of this that the Blessed One said, 'Any world … swept away'."

2. "Great king, do you, have chronic ailments? And can you command your kinsmen and others to share your painful feelings?" "No sir," said the king, "I have to feel that pain alone." Ratthapala explained, "It was on this account that the Blessed One said, 'Any world … no protector'."

3. "Great king, as you enjoy the five cords of sensual pleasure now, will you be able to have it of the life to come? 'Let me be likewise, or will others take over your wealth and do what they like with it?" "No sir, I cannot, others will take over my property." " It was on account of this that the Blessed One said, 'Any world has … and pass on'."

4. "Great king, do you reign over this rich Kuru country? And suppose someone tells you of a large country with more riches than here, with plenty of women for wives, would you want to conquer it?" "Why not sir!" replied the king, Ratthapala answered, "It was on this account that the Blessed One said, 'Any world is … of craving'."

Chapter Six
The Anatomy of Consciousness

The current, orthodox attitude of science to the question of consciousness is an obstacle to understand the Dhamma, particularly for medical men. Professor Sir Geoffrey Jefferson FRS writes, 'consciousness depends upon [or is the sum of] the activities of the whole intact nervous system', an elucidation of which, if complete, would give a proper understanding of it. He does not notice that 'to depend upon' and 'to be the sum of' are not the same thing. The mental qualities human beings display during consciousness is derived from nerve cells in the brain. This is the scientific view, and two assumptions are implicit:

1) There is a one-to-one relationship between each state of the nervous system and consciousness. Though a valid practical demonstration presents difficulties, I have no quarrel with it.

2) The nervous system obeys the laws of science, particularly of physics and biochemistry.

A physiologist has to make this second assumption: the laws of science are universal. Thus the biologist accepts laws established in chemistry and theoretical physics. The same experiment repeated at different times will always give the same result. Failure would lead to chaos. Should vaccination produce random effects—immunity in one, measles or a squint in another—medicine would become impossible. So, in view of the astonishing success of modern medicine, would anyone doubt this assumption?

Doubting this assumption does not necessarily lead to chaos. To deny the universality of science is not to deny there is any universal order. If there is a universal order more fundamental than revealed by science—which quantum theory in a muddled way is partly aware of—the scientist can be allowed a limited validity within it. Logicians take it that scientific laws are only probable and certainly not true. That is, the laws of science are less uniformly valid in one region than in another.

Is it necessary to doubt this assumption? Imagine that you rest your arm on a hot stove. You will immediately realise it. Why? You will say, the contact is painful. But that won't do. We need an account of the changes in the nervous system, strictly in scientific terms. Pain is not a scientific statement. An electrical impulse travelling up your nerve may be publicly recorded. But even in theory, the physiologist is unable to observe the pain you felt. If a nerve visible to a number of observers is stimulated, no two people can observe the same pain. Only the one who owns the nerve will experience it, undermining the hypothesis of the invariability of cause-and-effect for all observers at all times at all places, or pain is outside the scope of science. A physiologist can observe and record an impulse travelling up the arm, but not the pain. That is, he must make no reference to feeling [pleasure, pain,] and show his indifference to account for human behaviour. He must be able to account for lifting the arm from the stove strictly in terms of neural mechanisms alone without any reference to pain.

But fortunately, it was feeling that made him lift the arm otherwise, he might find the neural mechanism pressing it down further. By some happy chance, the body reacts to pleasure and pain. If we are to allow that feeling affects the state of the nervous system, raising the arm, we are obliged to abandon the universal validity of the laws of science. So long as feeling is dependent on the state of the nervous system and the state of the nervous system upon scientific determinism, all is well. But in addition, if the state of the nervous system is dependent on feeling, we enter the realms of scientific chaos. Feeling is not publicly observable. It is not a scientific entity and cannot be governed by any laws of science. The behaviour of the nervous system becomes wholly irrational, arbitrary. In short, the living body, and in particular, the nervous system are regions where the laws of science are not universally valid.

The achievements of the rational methods of science are striking and impressive. Rationalists make the irrational reason that science is capable of accounting for everything. Anyone challenging it meets with strong emotional reaction. Yet there is a failure of rational science that is still more striking. *And that is to account for itself.* Without the scientist there is no science. But science, in its claim to universal validity, cannot admit the existence of the scientist, a man who feels pain, since feeling is outside the domain of science. So a bastard entity is proposed: *sensation*—an electrical impulse travelling up a nerve, where under no circumstances can 'sensation' be taken to mean 'feeling'. But that is what it precisely means. By using it as if it was a physiological term, two incompatible meanings are fused in one word. Among other things, it is with this verbal legerdemain that the illusion of the 'universal validity of rational science' is maintained.

The current scientific interpretation of consciousness is itself inadequate quite apart from it being beyond the domain of science. Professor G Jefferson regards 'consciousness' to mean 'rational thought' or 'awareness' of what one is doing or thinking, and excluding thereby 'automatic or conditioned behaviour'. But conditioned behaviour [a rat learning from being made repeatedly uncomfortable with an electrical impulse] involves feeling. This restriction of consciousness to rational thought is a prejudice of rationalism. The Buddha specifically says that consciousness [*vinnana*], feeling [*vedana*] and perception [*sanna*] are inseparable. Whenever there is any one, all three are present. A subtle more intelligent approach is necessary to understand the Dhamma.

The mistake is to approach it by way of the body. Being public, rational science has no other way to study it except as matter. The laws of science are the laws of matter. But science overlooks the necessity that in order to know the body, it must first know what is consciousness instead of the other way around. Satre, in his principal work on consciousness running into seven hundred pages refers to the body after two hundred and fifty pages. ' … Now the body, whatever may be its function, appears first as the *known*. We cannot therefore refer knowledge back to it, or discuss it before we have defined *knowing*, nor can we derive knowing its fundamental structure from the body in any way or manner whatsoever.' And he points out that whatever we know about the body is derived from knowing about the bodies of other people. One does not know about his heart from having dissected it!

The Suttas put consciousness first and the body second. In the Dhamma, statements about *vinnana* are complex whereas about the body are simple. In the Dhamma, the mind comes first.

Notes

1. Satre, Jean Paul, *Being and Nothingness*, trs. by Hazel E. Barnes, London: Methuer, 1957; New York: Philosophical Library, 1957, *B & N*, p. 218

Chapter Seven

The Concept of Self in Dhamma

[*Composed from a 10-page letter written by
Nanavira Thera to his physician.*]

The 'doctrine of *anatta*' is the keystone in the arch of Dhamma—from *avijja* (nescience) at one end to *vijja* (science) at the other. After the passing away of the Buddha, the Brahmins attacked this position in its structure, leading to the collapse of the Dhamma in India. Yet, some posit even today that the Buddha was evasive on the subject.

The Dhamma has meaning only as a private experience for the wise. No aspect of the Dhamma can be fully understood and penetrated intellectually. No one not an *arahat* can fully 'see' or have insight of *anatta*, that is, have bodily and mental experience of it. No worldling can 'see' *anicca, dukkha, anatta*—the *tilakkhana* or three distinguishing marks of the Dhamma—all together at once—until one enters the path and reaps fruit or *sotapatti-phala*. That is why the Buddha did not 'explain' *anatta*.

There is a poignant incident in the Suttas concerning Rahula, when he was perhaps eighteen years old. One day, he joined the other bhikkhus to go on the alms round with the Buddha. The young Rahula saw the stately figure of his father leading the way and thought that he too is good-looking like him. The Buddha read his thoughts, looked back and said, "Rahula, any kind of material form, whatever, whether past, future, or present, internal or external, gross or subtle, inferior or superior, far or near, all material form should be seen as it actually is with proper wisdom thus: 'Not, this is mine; not, this am I; not, this is my self.'" "Only material form Blessed One?" meekly asked his son. "Material form, Rahula, and feeling, perception, determinations and consciousness," said the Buddha and continued on the alms round.

The statement 'N' *etam mama, n'esoham asmi, n' eso me atta*' runs through the Dhamma as a connecting thread; and it is commonly mistranslated as, 'This is not mine, this I am not, this is not my self'. Nanavira Thera translated it accurately: 'Not, this is mine; not, this am I; not, this is my self,' because the mistranslation implies, 'If this is not mine, then something *else* is mine.'

The concept of 'self' is often confused with the self of 'self-identity' [reflexion being different from reflection as explained later] and it is regarded as the basic principle of subjectivity. The *arahat* has surmounted the [false] belief in an unchanging self or soul but the *puthujjana* confuses [as the *arahat* does not] the self-identity of simple reflexion—as with a mirror, where the same thing is seen from two points of view at once ['the thing itself', 'the selfsame thing']– with the 'self' as the subject that appears in reflection: 'my self' [i.e. 'I itself', 'the I' that appears when I reflect].

The *puthujjana*, however does not see that attainment of *arahatta* removes all trace of the desire or conceit 'I am', leaving the entire reflective structure intact; in other words, that *subjectivity is a parasite on experience*[1].

The teaching of *anatta* is not difficult to state. Nanavira Thera overcame the compulsive belief in personality, the first fetter [*sakkayaditthi*], when he became a stream-entree and was thus able to give a masterly analysis from insight, from his private experience of release from 'belief in a self'. The discussion on *atta* or self is the most difficult chapter in the writings of Nanavira Thera. In the entire Dhamma, "The Discourse on the Not-Self Characteristic", the second teaching of the Buddha to the five ascetics, is the only Sutta *entirely* devoted to the subject of *anatta*.

The Buddha taught, "Bhikkhus, material form is not self. If material form were self, this material form would not lead to dukkha, and it could be had of material form: 'Let my material form be thus; let my material form be not thus.' And it is because material form is not self that it therefore leads to dukkha, and that it cannot be had of material form: 'Let my material form be thus; let my material form be not thus.'

"Feeling ... Perception ... Determinations ... are not self. Consciousness is not self. If consciousness were self, this consciousness would not lead to dukkha, and it could be had of consciousness: 'Let my consciousness be thus; let my consciousness be not thus.' And it is because consciousness is not self that it therefore leads to dukkha, and that it cannot be had of consciousness: 'Let my consciousness be thus; let my consciousness be not thus.'

"How do you conceive this? Is material form permanent or impermanent?" "Impermanent, Lord". "Is feeling ... consciousness, permanent or impermanent." "Impermanent, Lord". "But is it fitting to regard what is impermanent, unpleasant and subject to change – 'This is mine, this is what I am, this is my self?'" "No, Lord." "Therefore, any material form whatsoever ... consciousness whatsoever should all be regarded as it actually is by right understanding thus: 'Not, this is mine; not, this am I; not, this is my self.'"

This is the approach the Buddha takes everywhere in the Suttas to induce insight. What the Buddha essentially says can be rephrased in the following way: Do I have mastery over what I fondly regard is my very own material form ... consciousness? Do I have command over what I regard is my own material form ... consciousness? For example, can I command my body not to age, not to fall sick? Note that the apparent mastery you think you have of your 'self' is only welcome when things are pleasant and desired.

Mastery should not to be confused with the structure of reflective choice or intention [*cetana*] of the *puthujjana* and the *arahat*. 'The fact is that the intention or determination 'mine' pointing to a subject, is a complex structure involving *avijja* [nescience]... The Teaching of the Buddha of *anatta* has nothing whatsoever to do with self-identity: *anatta* is purely concerned with 'self' as subject', writes Nanavira Thera.

Aniccata in Dhamma [*sabbe sankhara anicca*] is about *subjective* impermanence, not the impermanence that we see around us. We do not require a Buddha to tell us urbanely that things in the world are impermanent. *Sabbe sankhara anicca* means that all conditioned things, all things upon which other things depend, so long as they point to a subject, appropriated by a self, are *aniccata*. When this is seen, all things, all dhamma, *sabbe dhamma anatta* follow. And when *sabbe sankhara dukkha* [all things upon which other things depend are suffering] is seen, *sabbe dhamma anatta* [all things that are not self] follow.

When the Buddha omitted the word *'sankhara'* in this third of the *tilakkhana*, it is commonly understood that since the *dhamma* includes Nibbana, he wanted to make clear that even Nibbana is without self. This is a complete misinterpretation. Nibbana is never referred either in terms of self or in terms of existence.

Consciousness [*vinnana*] is mere presence. But there cannot be presence without 'something' being present', writes Nanavira Thera. In terms of the Dhamma, this 'something' is name and matter [*namarupa*]. Together with *vinnana* it constitutes the phenomenon as a personal experience [in German: *Erlebnis*]. Thus *vinnana* and *namarupa* depend on each other. Consciousness is supported by name and matter, and vice versa.

'To be' and 'to be present' are the same thing. In terms of the Dhamma, 'being' as *bhava* involves the existence of the [illusory] subject. With the *arahat*, who has ceased to be a 'self', there is just 'presence'. This is 'seeing' with the Eye of Dhamma 'things actually as they are' [*yathabhuta nana.*] This is direct knowledge—without the intervention of a subject, without a reference point—totally absolute. For us [not *arahats*] there is nothing we can say about the world that is not relative to our self. Philosophers [and scientists] are permanently frustrated by this problem.

Read below the beautiful translation of Nanavira from *Le Mythe de Sisphe* by Albert Camus:

> Of whom and of what in fact can I say, 'I know about that!' This heart in me, I can experience it and I conclude that it exists. This world, I can touch it and I conclude again that it exists. All my knowledge stops there, and the rest is construction. For if I try to grasp this self of which I am assured, if I try to define it and to sum it up, it is no more than a liquid that flows between my fingers. I can depict one by one all the faces that it can assume; all those given to it, too, by this education, this origin, this boldness or these silences, this grandeur or this vileness. But one cannot add up faces. This same heart which is mine will ever remain for me undefinable. Between the certainty that I have of my existence and the content that I strive to give this assurance, the gap will never be filled. Always shall I be a stranger to myself … Here, again, are trees and I know their roughness, water and I experience its savour. This scent of grass and stars, night, certain evenings when the heart relaxes—how shall I deny this world whose power and forces I experience? Yet all the science on this earth will give me nothing that can assure me that this world is mine.

Nanavira Thera says, "a more lucid account by a *puthujjana* of his own predicament could scarcely be desired." He quotes Nietzche: 'The diligence of our best scholars, their senseless industry, their burning the candle of their brain at both ends—their very mastery of their handiwork—how often is the real meaning of all that to prevent themselves continuing to see a certain thing? Science as self-anesthetic: do you know that?'

Kant says it is a scandal of philosophy and human reason in general that there is no cogent proof for the 'being-there outside of us' that will do away with all skepticism. And Heidegger retorts by saying that the 'scandal of philosophy' is not that this proof has yet to be given, but that such proofs are expected and attempted again and again!

All thinkers, before and after the Buddha are frustrated by *avijja*, nescience; 'self' is a delusion of a delusion. The *arahat* has 'seen' it—and to 'him' things are never 'mine'. The panorama of experience, of happiness and sadness and equanimity, of all non-*arahat*s, are experiences interpreted as 'I have felt'. So, throughout the scenarios of existence, while things change, rise and fall, from birth to death, things are always felt, perceived and cognised by an unchanging same 'me', so long as there is *avijja*. That, as the central problem of dukkha, was the unique discovery of the Buddha.

Notes

1. Nanavira Thera, *Notes on Dhamma*, p. 54.

Chapter Eight

The Concept of Flux or Continuous Change

[Composed from a 10-page letter Venerable Nanavira Thera wrote in 1964. It is a brilliant demolition of the wrong notion of impermanence popularly taught in the Dhamma.]

Why am I so anxious to destroy the notion of flux or, at least, eliminate it from the context of the Dhamma? I have nothing to say against its proper use in science. But its proper place is not the Dhamma. Scientific thinking and the Dhamma belong to two different orders—as I hoped to have made plain in my Preface to *Notes on Dhamma*. The reason itself is to be found in your letter. You say, "The word flux means continuous change". If this idea is applied to everything it would be correct to say that what I see now, e.g. a tree, is not the same as I continue to watch it as it is subject to continuous change. Also, I have heard Buddhist monks saying, pointing to an object, "It is not there". This doctrine is a complete misunderstanding and is wholly misleading. In order to undermine this false doctrine, it is necessary to point out that the notion of flux, at least as applied to experience, is a self-contradiction.

But why is this false doctrine taught? It is because it provides a convenient simple interpretation of the Suttas [Discourses], easily learned and preached. The Buddha has said that 'What is impermanent, that is suffering; what is suffering is not-self'. This is misunderstood in the following way. Impermanence is taken to mean continuous change [flux] which if correct— the thing's continuing self-identity cannot be maintained—what *appears* to be the self-same tree persisting in time is not *really* the same since it is continuously changing. Consequently, the idea of *self* is an illusion. It is there because of *avijja,* or ignorance of the truth of universal flux. If we remove this ignorance, we shall see that what we formerly took to be a lasting or existing selfsame tree ['A =A', the principle of Self-identity] really has no abiding 'self' at all. It does not *really* exist. So what is wrong with that? What is wrong with it is that *it does not explain why what is impermanent is suffering, and what is suffering is not 'self'.*

The concept of 'suffering' [dukkha] is the key to the whole of the Buddha's Teaching, and any interpretation that leaves it out—or adds it as an afterthought—is at once suspected. Suffering has nothing to do with a tree's self-identity or supposed lack of it. What it *does* have to do with is, *my* 'self' as subject [I, ego], which is quite another matter. I have pointed out elsewhere that with the question of a thing's self-identity [which presents no difficulty] the Buddha's Teaching of *anatta* has nothing whatsoever to do. *Anatta* is purely concerned with 'self' as '*subject*'. But this is more difficult to grasp than the misinterpretation based on the notion of flux, so flux gets the popular vote. The misinterpretation is actually of Mahayana origin. In one of their texts [*Prajnaparamita*] it is specifically stated that it is on account of *avijja* [nescience] that things appear to exist, whereas in *reality* nothing exists. But the fact is that even for an *arahat* a tree continues to have a self-identity. It continues to exist as the *same* tree until it dies or is cut down. But for the *arahat* it is no longer '*my* tree' since all notions of 'I' and 'mine' have ceased.

The 'Gestalt' school of psychology has specialised in experimental investigation of perception of change, and has reported that every change we perceive takes place suddenly and absolutely. Whenever perception of change is described as 'taking place continuously', it is to be presumed either that the analysis of a complex experience is beyond the power of the perceiver, or rationalisation has taken place. That in fact we have experience of movement is not to be denied. These experiences are notoriously difficult to describe. The problem of movement has puzzled philosophers from time immemorial. The starting point of any discussion of motion is Zeno's Eleatic arrow. Bertrand Russell gives some account of this celebrated paradox but the problem is not so easily solved as he thinks [*M & L*, pp. 79-83]. The solution described by Russell solves the problem by leaving it out! The problem is: *What is time?*

The word flux means flowing. That is, continuous change. The Oxford dictionary defines it as 'a continuous succession of changes'— change one after another with no interval of time between these changes. How much time does a single change take? Either it takes some time, in which case we are obliged to say that each individual change is a continuous change and therefore itself a flux; or it takes no time and is instantaneous, in which case we have to conclude that a flux is itself instantaneous, since there is no time *between* the changes. You cannot have a *succession* of changes – one change after another – if *no* time is involved. To say that every individual change is a flux, makes the definition circular, and we still do not know what a flux is!

Let us take a slice of 'flux' and divide it into three consecutive sections A, B, C. Note that we cannot take three consecutive *instants* without falling into contradiction since instants, which are of *no* time, cannot be consecutive, i.e. both contiguous and successive. We are forbidden to introduce the idea of an individual change. So, 'A = B' and 'B = C'. If we postulate that A and B [or B and C] are *both* contiguous *and* different we define a discrete individual change—there is 'a change' at the junction of A and B where A changes to B. But a flux is a *change* and we must introduce the idea of *difference*—say, 'A is different from C'. Since A and C are not contiguous we have not defined any discontinuous change between them and all is well. Between A and C there is *change* but not *a change*. So A = B, B = C and A is different to C which agrees with the notion of flux as applied to any section of flux. But alas, there is a self-contradiction! B = C [or C = B] and A is different to C; therefore A is different to B; but also A = B; therefore both A = B and A is different to B. This outrages the law of contradiction: 'A is not both B and not-B'.

Arising, disappearance and change while persisting applies to all experience, physical objects or states of mind [not included in science]. Moreover, the notion of flux, I maintain, cannot also be applied to physical objects. The structure of changes of mental states such as pleasure and grief 'appear and vanish and reappear'. But is this also not true of physical objects? Do we not have familiar sights, sounds, smell, tastes and bodily contacts? Arising, disappearing and *change while persisting* apply to *all* experience. This last, characteristic *thitassa annathattam,* as I understand, expresses the combination of absolute sameness and absolute difference. This is the essential structure of all change. [Elsewhere, Nanavira refers to the famous epigram of Hereclitus and notes that a pupil of Hereclitus said, 'You cannot step into the same river even once!' *If everything is changing, there is no change.*]

The idea of continuous change is not a matter of observation. It is a theoretical assumption arising from the scientific claim to complete objectivity. Science aims at eliminating the observer, the individual point of view. As soon as the observer is reinstated as in quantum theory, change becomes discontinuous. "The *puthujjana*", says the Buddha, "has the habit of treating the body as the necessary basis for all his inferences". The existential view too is that, for an individual, the world necessarily presents itself in one perspective or another. The scientist or scholar, on principle, wants to know nothing of self and its inseparable correlative, the world. But the world is nothing other than that which is determined by each of us with reference to the self, though there are common similarities. The collection of independent public facts of the scientific method is inherently incapable, says Nanavira Thera, of constituting a world since it lacks a unifying personal determinant—which is the aim of science to eliminate. Things, not facts, *pace* Wittgenstein, make up my world, writes Nanavira Thera in the Preface to his book *Notes on Dhamma*.

When the infant grows into a man, we see that the infant has changed. We say the infant both is and is not the same as the man. In order to say 'this has changed' two things are necessary: (i) sameness, and (ii) not-sameness, or difference. Unless there is something that remains the same, we cannot say 'this'; and unless there is something that is different, we cannot say 'changed'. Leaving aside the case when one sensible quality varies while another remains constant [a leaf turning into shades of green], it is always the case that the more **general** feature [greenness of the leaf] remains invariable while it is the subordinate or **particular** that varies. That is, there is a structure of change—as stated by the Buddha—and the statement 'everything is changing' needs strict qualification. He says that there are serious objections to introducing this notion of flux from scientific contexts into the Dhamma.

In a discussion of *Invariance under Transformation* [found in quantum theory and the theory of groups in mathematics] Nanavira Thera says that the dialectic he has constructed in 'Fundamental Structure' [See *Notes on Dhamma*] is 'capable of completely describing discontinuous changes at different levels of generality'.

Chapter Nine

Consciousness and Rebirth

The subject of consciousness is under intense research by neuro-physiologists, biochemists and even physicists. In the Dhamma, it is not described in arcane, esoteric terms of these sciences or philosophy. Philosophers and scientists shall probably never 'uncover' it because it is impossible to be conscious of consciousness. In the Dhamma analysis, consciousness pervades the body and mind of all living beings. It cannot be syringed out for examination like blood! And there is no recognition of Freudian and Jungian states of subconscious and unconsciousness. In higher meditative absorptions, the Buddha refers access to 'infinite consciousness', which is experienced by the meditator.

In the body, which is the sole concern in the Dhamma, consciousness is regarded as an element [*dhatu*]. "Bhikkhu, this person consists of six elements. So it was said. And with reference to what was this said? There are the earth element, the water element, the fire element, the air element, the space element and the consciousness element," said the Buddha to

Venerable Pukkusati when the two of them spent one night in a potters shed [M 140]. The space element, Buddha declares, has however no standing of its own. It is just space of the ear-hole, nose, etc. When the walls and roofs of a house are built, it encloses space. In higher meditative states, the Buddha speaks of the additional of experience of 'infinite space'.

Why does one say 'consciousness'? It cognises, that is why it is called consciousness. Cognises what? It cognises, for example, tastes like sour, bitter, pungent, sweet, alkaline, not-alkaline, salty and not-salty. 'Consciousness is reckoned by the particular condition dependent upon which it arises—just as fire is reckoned by the particular condition dependent on which it burns.' 'Consciousness is called after the conditions due to which it arises. When consciousness arises due to eye and forms, it is called eye-consciousness; due to ear and sounds, ear-consciousness; due to nose and smells, nose-consciousness; due to tongue and tastes, tongue-consciousness; due to body and touch, body-consciousness; due to mind and ideas, mind-consciousness ...' What does that consciousness cognise? It cognises, for example, that there is pleasure, that there is pain, that there is neither-pain-nor-pleasure. Feeling, perception and consciousness are conjoined, not disjoined, and it is impossible to separate the other from each in order to describe their potentialities.

Consciousness depends for its being upon a duality—the duality of the in oneself and the external bases for contact [form, sound, smell, taste, touch, ideas]. Any consciousness whatever, whether past, future or present, in oneself or external, coarse or fine, inferior or superior, far or near, that is affected by taints and provocative of holding: that is called the conscious aggregate of holding. What is called 'mentality' and 'mind' and consciousness arises and ceases differently through the night and day, just as a monkey ranging through the forest seizes a branch, and letting that go seizes another'.

In the *Mahanidana* Sutta of the Digha Nikaya [as translated by Nanavira Thera] the Buddha says, "With consciousness as condition, name-and-matter [*nama-rupa*], so it was said: how it is, Ananda, that consciousness as condition there is name-and-matter should be seen in this manner. If, Ananda, consciousness were not to descend into the mother's womb, would name-and-matter be consolidated in the mother's womb?" "No indeed, lord." "If Ananda, having descended into the mother's womb, consciousness were to turn aside, would name-and-matter be delivered into this situation?" "No indeed, lord." "If, Ananda, consciousness were cut off from one still young, from a boy or a girl, would name-and-matter come to increase, growth, and fullness?" "No indeed, my lord." "Therefore, Ananda, just this is the reason, this is the occasion, this is the arising, this is the condition of name-and-matter, that is to say consciousness ... If, Ananda, consciousness were not to obtain a stay in name-and-matter, would future arising and coming-into-being of birth, aging, death, and *dukkha* be manifest?" "No indeed, lord." "Thus far, Ananda, may one be born or age or die or fall or arise, thus far is there a way of designation, thus far is there a way of language, thus far is there a way of description, thus far is there a sphere of understanding, thus far the round proceeds as manifestation in a situation, so far, that is to say, as there is name-and-matter together with consciousness."

In the *Mahatanhasankhaya* Sutta of the Majjhima Nikaya, the Buddha reprimands bhikkhu Sati for saying, "As I understand the Dhamma taught by the Blessed One, it is the same consciousness that runs and wanders through the round of rebirths, not another." "Misguided man, in many discourses have I not stated consciousness to be dependently arisen, since without a condition there is no origination of consciousness?" The Buddha says that from one rebirth to another three kinds of acquisitions of 'self' can succeed another. "The gross material form consists of the four great entities and consumes physical food. The second has fine material form and is constituted by mind with all its limbs [feeling, perception, intention] lacking no faculty. The third is formless and consists only perception … I teach the Dhamma for abandoning all acquisitions of 'self' … it cannot be successfully argued that only one of them is true and the others wrong. One can only say that the term for any one does not fit the other. Just as with milk from a cow, curd from milk, butter from curd, ghee from butter, and fine extract of ghee from ghee, the term of each fits only that and none of the others, yet they are not disconnected … These are worldly usages, worldly language, worldly terms of communication, worldly descriptions by which a Perfect One communicates without misapprehending them."

On 'sameness', Nanavira Thera quotes Bradley from his book *Principles of Logic*. 'It takes two to make the same, and the least we can have is some change of event in a self-same thing, or return to that thing from some suggested difference.' Nonetheless, the *Milindapanha*, a highly regarded ancient Dhamma text has established the dictum '*Na ca so na ca anno*' ['Neither he nor another'] as the answer to the question: 'When a man dies, who is reborn—he or another?' Nanavira Thera writes, 'This question is illegitimate because it takes for granted the validity of the belief in 'self' or personality [*sakkayaditthi*]. It follows that any answer takes 'self' for granted, since it allows the question to be asked. The proper way is to reject the question'. So long as there is nescience [*avijja*] and craving [*tanha*], the idea of 'self' is affectively produced. The man who sees a mirage [a delusion] thinks it is real [a delusion]. The 'self' likewise, is a delusion of a delusion.

The Buddha teaches that when a 'being' dies holding to nescience and craving, there is 'coming to be of a further being' [*punnabbavabhinibbati*]. Strictly, it is said, a Pali word corresponding to 're-birth' is avoided in the Suttas. What is relevant here is not the word but the indicated meaning: There is no 'become' to 're-become'. The complete state of holding—belief in 'self and its more subtle 'I-am'— [*attavada-upadana*] is extirpated only by the *arahat*—which is the aim of striving in the Dhamma. For this reason, when referring to the 'living' *arahat* the words 'birth' and 'death' are avoided [*Kosala Samyutta*]. Strictly, it cannot be said that the Buddha was not born, and it cannot be said he died. The 'person' born was Siddharata Gotama, and the 'individual' that passed away finally was Gotama Buddha, never to re-appear. The distinction between 'person' and 'individual' is critical.

Notes

1. Any phenomenon present in consciousness has two characteristics—inertia and designation [*patigha* and *adhivacana*]. Inertia is *rupa* or form or matter, which may be seen as also its behaviour. This presents itself only in the passage of time. The

four modes of behaviour of matter [*mahabhuta*] are: earthy or ripening or solid; watery or cohesive; fiery or ripening; airy or distended or moving. *Nama* means designation or name. It is commonly and wrongly understood as mind. *Nama* is usefully understood as appearance. Thus, matter or *rupa* cannot be said to exist by itself. It must first appear and be named. The Buddha defines *nama* as consisting of feeling [*vedana*], pleasant, unpleasant or neutral; perception or percepts [*sanna*] of perception of form, taste, smell, sound, touch, ideas; significance or intention [*cetana*]; engagement in experience or contact [*phassa*]; and selective or intentional direction of attention [*manasikara*]. Thus, *nama* is the appearance of *rupa*; and *rupa* is the behaviour of *nama* [condensed from Nanavira Thera.] All *arahat*s, as it were, have de-coupled the *nama*-body from *rupa*.

In the Dhamma, there is no state of 'unconscious and sub-conscious'. Even in sleep, we are conscious, otherwise a sudden sound, for example, cannot wake us. Reflex action is mere movement, like a stone rolling down a slope. The consciousness of the *arahat* is different from that of the *puthujjana*. There has been so to say, a metamorphosis. It is spoken as being *anidassana* – non-indicative, not pointing to a self. In the uninstructed commoner, stimuli streaming into consciousness through the five senses and mind make contact with the illusory self, but for the uninstructed, his real self, and the impact is interpreted in diverse ways – mine, my view, inference, likes and dislikes, adherence, inclination, etc. This is not 'seeing things as they actually are' but through reference to the self.

'This world is subject to torment; afflicted by contact, it calls a disease 'self'. For however it is conceived, it is ever otherwise than that [Udana 3.10]. 'To know is to uncover craving; to see is to have done with owning' [Udana 8:1-3]. 'I am is derivative, not underivative. Derivative upon what? Derivative upon form, feeling, perception, determinations and consciousness [S 22.83]. 'It would be better for an untaught ordinary man to treat as self this body, which is constructed upon the four great entities, than *nama*. Why? Because this body can last one year, two years ... hundred years; but what is called 'mentality' and 'mind' and consciousness arises and ceases differently through night and day, just as a monkey ranging through the forest seizes a branch, and letting it go, seizes another' [S 12.61]. 'Form is like a lump of froth; feelings like a water bubble; perception too is like a mirage; determinations like a plantain trunk [just sheaves and no core]; and consciousness seems nothing but a conjuring trick' [S 22.95].

Chapter Ten
Mindfulness and Awareness

There are three Suttas to indicate the practice of awareness [*sampajanna*] in the Dhamma: 1. 'Here monks, in walking to and fro, a monk practises awareness; in looking ahead and looking aside he practises awareness ... 2. Here, monks, feelings are known when they arise, feelings are known as they endure, feelings are known as they vanish; perceptions are known ... thoughts are known ... as they vanish. 3. Here, Ananda, a monk is mindful as he walks, he is mindful as he walks to and fro, he is mindful as he stands, he is mindful as he sits, he is mindful as he sets to work. This, Ananda, is a mode of recollection that, when developed and made much of in this way, leads to mindfulness-awareness [*satisampajanna*.]

Mindfulness is general recollectedness, not being scatter-brained whereas awareness means *keeping oneself under constant observation*, not letting actions, thoughts, feelings, etc, rise and fall unnoticed. Habitual actions are done without thinking, such as blinking the eyes, scratching the head. They are not 'unconscious' actions. The Buddha defined action [*kamma*] as intention [*cetana*]. The so-called unconscious action is simply a movement like that of a stone rolling down a slope. In the Dhamma, all actions of the mind, speech and body are conscious actions. A conscious action is deliberate. It requires thought to perform. Considering what we are doing is what constitutes awareness. It is sometimes thought that it is not possible to do two things at the same time. What is not possible is to give *equal* attention [*manasikara*] to them. So long as we are awake, there is some degree of awareness of most things we do. We are obliged to consider what we are doing. Awareness is in abeyance when we dream. A nightmare is a struggle to wake up, trying to remember or become aware that we are dreaming. But when awake, we are absorbed in what we are doing—in affection, lust, boredom, hate and so on. We however keep awareness to a minimum. But we cannot avoid it altogether. Generally, we become aware in order to get through routine things expeditiously.

In the Dhamma, awareness has a different purpose. It is practised to get a *release from living*. The Buddha says that three things harm the progress of a bhikkhu under training: fondness for work [sewing robes, sweeping, etc], fondness for talk and fondness for sleep. When going to sleep, a bhikkhu is required to bear in mind the time to wake up. He is required to always act mindfully and with awareness. Drive and initiative are regarded as impediments to progress in the Dhamma.

How does one practise awareness for release? All that is necessary is a slight change of attitude, a slight change of effort and attention. Instead of being fully absorbed or involved in what we are doing, without ceasing to act, *observe* what we are doing and thinking. Ask, "What am I doing? What am I thinking"? And we must go on asking this question until observing whatever we are doing or thinking becomes automatic. But why practise mindfulness and awareness? There are three good reasons. It develops virtue [*sila*], concentration [*samadhi*] and wisdom [*panna*]. It develops self-criticism. It gives a powerful control over the passions and constant practice inhibits passions or they arise less frequently.

The practice of *satisampajanna* is an absolute pre-requisite for understanding the essence of the Dhamma. The reason is that the Dhamma is not concerned with this or that experience but with *all* experiences in general. We do not need a Buddha to tell us how to cope with a particular feeling, say a headache or anger. We need a Buddha to tell us how to escape from *all* experiences whatsoever. When we are aware of what we are doing or feeling or thinking, we are observing it with detachment. This is *reflexion* as opposed to *reflection*. In reflexion, the immediate experience is observed. That is, it is watched or considered *twice*. This is *sampajanna*, awareness. While reflection or introspection includes reflexion, there is no reflection in reflexion. In reflexion, there is certainty of the present. In reflection, there can be error. When we observe things with detachment, with dispassion, we become aware of the *general* nature of things or experience—impermanent, changing, fading, *dukkha*. We become aware of the universal nature of phenomena. And with guidance from the Buddha, we are able to surmount *all* experiences, gradually and progressively.

The Buddha regarded the body as a 'disease' but a statement, 'Health is the greatest wealth' [*arogya parama labha*] is widely misinterpreted. 'Then at that point the Blessed One uttered this exclamation: "The greatest of all gains is health, Nibbana is the greatest bliss ... " Then the wanderer Magandiya said he too had heard of the saying. "But Magandiya, when you heard that said by earlier wanderers in the tradition of the teachers, what is that health, what is that Nibbana?" When this was said, Magandiya rubbed his limbs with his hands and said, "This is that health, Master Gotama, this is that Nibbana; for I am healthy and happy and nothing affects me". The Buddha then said, "Now it [the stanza] has gradually become current among ordinary people. And although this body, Magandiya, is a disease, a tumor, a dart, a calamity, and an affliction, you say ... You do not have that noble vision, Magandiya, by means of which you might know health and see Nibbana." From that point, the Buddha gave Magandiya a discourse on *mental health*. [Condensed from M 75]

A Zen master says, "When I eat, I eat. When I sleep, I sleep". The meaning is that he is fully mindful and aware, focussing attention exclusively on the present. "Let not a person revive the past" says the Buddha, "or on the future build his hopes; for the past has been left behind and the future has not been reached. Instead with insight let him see each presently arisen state; let him know that and be sure of it, invincibly, unshakably. Today the effort must be made; tomorrow, Death may come, who knows?" [M 131] My favourite quotation is the teaching of the ascetic Bahiya who realised he was not an *arahat* as he had assumed and travelled a long way to meet the Buddha. He met him during an alms round and then and there, on road, begged, "Sugata, please teach the Dhamma". "It is an unsuitable time, Bahiya, we have entered among houses for almsfood." But Bahiya implored for a third time. Then, seeing that he was a wise man, standing on the road, instantly, the Buddha gave what can be regarded as the supreme gist of his teaching. "*Herein, Bahiya, you should train yourself thus: In the seen will be merely what is seen; in the heard will be merely what is heard; in the sensed will be merely what is sensed; in the cognised is merely what is cognised. In this way you should train yourself.*" [See 'Words of Wisdom' for the rest of the teaching.] Here, as everywhere, in the Dhamma, mindfulness and awareness is the basis upon which a person is enjoined to train to gain insight. The Dhamma is not an anodyne for any particular experience. It is a gradual training that leads to insight of *anicca, dukkha and anatta.*

Chapter Eleven
Practice of Meditation in Dhamma

In recent times, meditation has become a very popular sought after practice worldwide. The WHO, the medical profession and psychiatrists have accepted it for treating depression, bio-feedback to control high blood pressure, for other therapeutic purposes, for jaded businessmen, and so on. Some so-called Meditation Masters make it a thriving business. All of this has nothing to with the Dhamma. Meditation as understood and thus used is not the purpose for which the Buddha taught it more than 2,500 years ago.

To begin with, the word meditation is a generic term for a mental discipline taught and practised very likely in India firstly by the *rishis*, saints who claim to have 'received knowledge', about 3,000 years ago. It spread perhaps 'rapidly' along the Silk Route and after Alexander invaded Northern India. The Buddha learnt *anapanasati* or mindfulness of in and out breathing from two of the foremost masters of the day to attain serenity or *samadhi*, or one-pointedness of mind. This is *samadhi bhavana*, the distinguishing feature of which is that the mind is trained to focus *only one object*, either the in-and-out breath, or a red disc, or a handful of earth, or a flower. In this way, the Buddha taught forty methods of *samadhi* [*samatha*, serenity, tranquillity] meditation. It was well-known and popular in the time of the Buddha. So there is little detail description of it in the Dhamma. As Nanavira Thera puts it, fish do not need instructions from a swimming teacher. Variations of the technique are found in Hinduism, Christianity, Islam, Sufism, etc. The 'spin-off' effects can be experienced in diverse ways and situations.

The *bhavana* that is unique in the Dhamma is *vipassana* or insight meditation the aim and essence of which is to reach the pinnacle of wisdom or *panna* or *sammaditthi* [right view] of the Dhamma. It may come as a surprise for many devotees to realise that nowhere has the Buddha recommended group meditation, as practised today at episodic '10 day-retreats'. At the end of many discourses to disciples in training [*sekha*], he says as here, "What should be done for his disciples out of compassion by a teacher who seeks their welfare and has compassion for them, that I have done for you, Cunda. There are these roots of trees, these empty huts. Meditate, Cunda, do not delay or else you will regret later. This is our instruction to you" [M 8.17].

In *samadhi* meditation, whatever object is chosen to focus and concentrate the mind, the principle is achieving one-pointedness concentrating only on *one* object, at any *one* time. In *vipassana bhavana*, any number of 'things' [*dhamma*] that come to awareness [*sampajanna*] by the six doors—eye, ear, nose, tongue, body, mind—can become the object of meditation. Now one may even wonder if this is meditation!

Development of wisdom, through *vipassana* is a sine qua non for final liberation [*vimutti*]. Both should be practised yoked together like cart bulls until one is *skilled* in both forms. This is the state of developed and cultivated mindfulness and awareness [*satisampajanna*]. Essentially, to practise Dhamma is to be in this mode, to examine, accept and interpret experience in Dhamma-terms, with wisdom. The purpose of wisdom says Sariputta, "is direct knowledge [*abhinna*]. Its purpose is full understanding [*parinna*], and its purpose is abandoning [*pahana*]". The Buddha advised a bhikkhu, Meghiya thus: " When mind-deliverance is as yet immature, Meghiya, five things lead to maturity. What five? Here, Meghiya, a bhikkhu has good friends and companions; is virtuous, seeing danger in the smallest faults; obtains at will, with no trouble or difficulty in opening the mind to talk that is effacing [*sallekha*], leading to dispassion, cessation; lives with energy for abandoning unwholesome states; is wise, endowed with the noble one's penetrative understanding. These five things, Meghiya, lead to maturity of mind-deliverance. … A bhikkhu, Meghiya, who is established in these five things should also cultivate four additional things: perception of foulness [*asubhasanna*] for overcoming lust [*raga*]; loving-kindness [*metta*] for overcoming malevolence [*vyapada*]; respiration-mindfulness [*anapanasati*] for cutting off [discursive] thinking; the perception of impermanence [*aniccata*] for removal of the conceit 'I am'. For when one perceives impermanence, Meghiya, the perception of not-self is established [*sabbe dhamma anatta*]. When one perceives not-self one reaches the removal of the conceit 'I-am', which is called Nibbana here and now". [Condensed from Udana 4.1]

The magnum opus of the Dhamma on meditation, the *Satipatthana* Sutta, was taught to a group of monks, probably in his early years when the Buddha could walk perhaps 500 miles, at a town in the Kuru country, near modern Delhi. He began the talk, "Bhikkhus this way leads only to the purification of beings …" "[*Ekayano ayam bhikkhave maggo sattam visuddhiya* …" [M 10, D 22]. Regrettably, these words of the Buddha are misinterpreted and mistranslated as 'The only way' 'the direct path', as if there is an indirect path! Nanavira Thera, makes an acute observation and writes: "Actually, the 'only way' leading to *nibbana* is the noble eight-factored path [*ariyo atthangiko maggo*], of which *satipatthana* is only one of the factors [the seventh]".

In this difficult discourse, the Buddha summarises the way mindfulness is developed as the basis for progress. "Here bhikkhus, this way leads only to the purification of beings, for the surmounting of sorrow and lamentation, for the disappearance of pain and grief, for the attainment of the true way, for realisation of Nibbana, namely, the four stations of mindfulness. What four? Here, a bhikkhu abides contemplating the body as a body [*kayanupassana*], ardent, fully aware, and mindful, having put away covetousness [*abhijja*] and grief for the world. He abides contemplating feelings as feelings [*vedananupassana*] ardent, fully aware, and mindful, having put away covetousness and grief for the world. He abides contemplating mind as mind [*cittanupassana*], ardent, fully aware, and mindful, having put away covetousness and grief for the world. He abides contemplating mind-objects as mind-objects [*dhammanupassana*] ardent, fully aware, and mindful, having put away covetousness and grief for the world."

The Buddha next outlines the following components: mindfulness of breathing [*anapanasati*], the four postures [*iriyapatha*], full awareness [*satisampajanna*], foulness of body parts [*patikulamanasikara*], elements [*dhatumanasikara*], the nine cemetery contemplations [*navassivathika*], contemplation of feeling, mind, the five hindrances [*nivarana*], the five aggregates [*panc'upanakkhanda*] the six bases [*salayatana*], the seven enlightenment factors [*bojjhanga*], and finally, the four noble truths [*aryasacca*] in that order. He concludes with a flourish, "Bhikkhus, if anyone should develop *satipatthana* in such a way for seven years ... for six years ... for five years ... for four years ... for three years ... for two years ... for one year ... for seven months ... for six months ... four five months ... for four months ... for three months ... for two months ... for one month ... for half a month ... for seven days, one of the two fruits [*phala*] could be expected for him: either final knowledge here and now, or if there is a trace of holding [*upadana*] left, non-return [*anagami*]. Further development and cultivation leads to Nibbana, here and now".

The Buddha says, that *anapanasati* [meditation on the in and out breathing] fulfils the four *satipatthana* and expounded on the origin and disappearance of *satipatthana* thus: 'The body has nutriment [*ahara*] for its origin and it disappears with cessation of nutriment; feelings have contact as their origin and it disappears with the cessation of contact; consciousness has name and matter for its origin and disappears with cessation of name and matter; mental objects have attention [*manasikara*] for their origin and disappear with cessation of attention.'

He taught his son Rahula thus: Develop meditation on loving-kindness [*metta*] to abandon ill-will [*vyapada*]; develop meditation on compassion [*karuna*] to abandon cruelty [*himsa*]; develop meditation on appreciative joy [*mudita*] to abandon discontent, develop meditation on equanimity [*upekkha*] [1] to abandon aversion [*dosa*]; develop meditation on foulness to abandon lust [*raga*]; develop meditation on perception of impermanence [*aniccata*] to abandon the conceit 'I-am' [*asmi mana*]; develop meditation on mindfulness of breathing, which when developed and cultivated, it is of great fruit and benefit. The Buddha concluded the discourse, "Rahula ... when *anapanasati* is developed and cultivated in this way, even the final in-breaths and out-breaths are known as they cease, not unknown." [M 62]

To meditate in the Buddha's Dispensation it is imperative to learn the true Dhamma in order to succeed in it. Nanavira Thera expounds on the subject[2]. 'As regards *samadhi*, the situation is this. As soon as a person reaches the first path [not the fruition, which may come much later], he gets the *ariyapuggala's* right view [*sammaditthi*], which is his *panna* [wisdom]. And it is characteristic of *panna* that when one has it [as an *aryapuggala*] one also has *samadhi* [concentration], *viriya* [energy], *saddha* [virtue], and *sati* [mindfulness]'[3]. In a footnote, he says: 'This fact is not understood by the *puthujjana*, who has no experience of such a phenomenon. Certainly he can get *samadhi* of a kind [by the practice of *ananpanasati*, for example], but this is not the *sammasamadhi* of the path [which he does not have]. And similarly with *viriya*, *saddha* and *sati*'.

Another misunderstood type of *bhavana* is *metta bhavana*, which is widely regarded as easy and is done sometimes as a political stunt to radiate loving-kindness to enemies and friends. First and foremost, it is developed and cultivated by skilled disciples to obtain *jhana*. For others, the Buddha recommended it as a way to get rid of anger. Normally, anger arises when dealing with people and *metta* is best practised before dealing with other people. But first, it is necessary to know what *metta* is, and secondly, have it at our command. Just as it is not difficult to practise *ananpanasati* in the presence of others *when you are skilled in it, metta bhavana* is possible when you have developed and cultivated *skill* in it. Just as the worst possible condition for *anapanasati* is presence of other people, one can never succeed in *metta bhavana* except in *solitude*. Noise and bustle is a hindrance to *bhavana*. The obstacles are too great to overcome. For example, if there is someone you dislike in whose presence you get angry, unless you are able to prevent anger from arising when that person is *absent* which needs a lot of practice, you shall have no chance of getting rid of arisen anger when the person is *present*. There is not much that you can now do except stop it from taking possession of you by say, with harsh words. It is now far too late to practise *metta bhavana*. That is, *metta bhavana should be practised in solitude until you are skilled in it.*

The point to note is that while *anapanasati* concerns yourself, your breathing, *metta* is about other people. To learn and acquire skill in *metta bhavana*, the *bodies* of other people are redundant, nay a hindrance. It is not other **people** that are a hindrance to practise *metta bhavana*, it is their **bodies**. This subtle point cannot be over emphasised. In short, *metta* is best at a distance from its object. In the Suttas for protection from snakes, one first develops thoughts of *metta* to all beings, leg-less, two-legged, four-legged, and many legged.

Metta bhavana is difficult. To regard it easy is naïve. A socialist or a do-gooder may delude himself that he has *metta* or love for the whole of humanity. But 'humanity' is an abstraction—'humanity' as a whole can neither be hated nor loved. The communist is wont to regard each individual an enemy of the 'people'. *Metta bhavana is about loving all individual beings, starting with oneself*[4].

Notes

1. *Metta, karuna, mudita*, and *upekkha* are known as the *brahmavihara* or the four sublime abodes.

2. Nanavira Thera, *Writings of Nanavira Thera,* vol 2, 'Letters', p. 219. He says that the wrong translation 'is preferred by people who write about *satipatthana* since it gives an added importance to their subject!'

3. *Saddha, viriya, sati, samadhi* and *panna* are known as five faculties [*indriya* and the same again, as *bala* or power] developed by the *ariyasavaka* [noble disciple] and totally absent in the *puthujjana*. They are the power and strength of the noble disciple, as equipment, to practise the Dhamma. It is the task of the *puthujjana* to *acquire* them—they are not even latent in him.

4. Adapted from the writings of Nanavira Thera.

Chapter Twelve
The Laws of Thought

All thinking in defiance of the Laws of Thought [from Poincare] is *frivolous*, asserts Nanavira Thera. They are stated as —

(a) Identity: 'A is A'[1],

(b) Contradiction: 'A is not both B and not B',

(c) Excluded Middle: 'A is either B or not B'.

The rationalist says that his thinking conforms to these laws and there is no problem. But the present state of scientific thinking—which claims to be rational thinking par excellence—shows that rational thinking is maintained by introducing extraordinary absurdities into its premises. Eddington assumed that 'exactly as many things exist as do not exist'. This is good currency in quantum theory. Now physicists postulate a *'partly non-existent thing'*. PAM Dirac, Lucassian Professor of Mathematics, University of Cambridge, in his book, *The Principles of Quantum Mechanics* says: "The important things in the world appear as the invariants [or more generally the nearly invariant] of these transformations." A *thing* as an invariant is in order—A is A. But a nearly invariant is a quasi-identity—A is nearly A or, *almost* a thing. Only *things* can be stated to exist and '*almost a thing*' is the same as saying 'partly non-existent thing'.

The rationalist does not see any problem to be solved, not because his thinking conforms to the Laws of Thought. On the contrary, he turns a blind eye to the fact that *his thinking is based on the violations of the Laws of Thought*. The problem certainly is there for the *puthujjana* by persistent refusal to disregard the Laws of Thought [*puthujjana* = uninstructed common man.] The existentialist philosopher on the other hand handles the problem differently—he examines and describes his own thinking in an act of reflexion, obstinately refusing to tolerate non-identities, contradictions and excluded middles. But at a certain point he comes up against a contradiction that he cannot resolve. It is seen to be inherent in his very act of thinking. *This contradiction is the existence of the thinker himself* [*as subject*] *or 'self'*.

This contradiction is presented more concisely in the later part of the *Maha Nidana Sutta* [*Digha Nikaya* 15, ii, 66-8] where the Buddha says that a man who identifies his 'self' with feeling should be asked which kind of feeling—pleasant, unpleasant or neutral, does he regard as his 'self'. The man cannot identify his 'self' with all three kinds of feelings at once, since only one of the three kinds is present at a time. If he does make this identification, therefore, he must do it with the three different kinds of feelings, in *succession*. His 'self', of course, is taken for granted as self-identical by him—'A is A'—that is to say, as the *same* 'self' on each occasion. This he proceeds to identify in turn with the three *different* feelings: B, C, and D A is therefore both B and C [not to mention D]; and C, being different from B, is not B: so A is both B and not B—a violation of the Law of Contradiction. But whether or not it is with feeling that the *puthujjana* is identifying 'self', he is always identifying it with *something*, and it is a *different* something on each occasion. The *puthujjana* takes his existence for granted—*cogito ergo sum* [which, as Satre says, is apodictic reflexive evidence of the thinker's existence]—and is in a perpetual state of contradiction.

Assuming the validity of the Laws of Thought, the thinker discovers that the whole of his thinking depends upon an irreducible violation of the Laws of Thought, namely *the contradictory existence of the thinker. And this itself is a contradiction.* If he tolerates it, he denies the validity of the Laws of Thought whose validity he assumed when he established the contradiction in the first place. There is therefore no contradiction for him to tolerate, and consequently he is not denying the Laws of Thought. The contradiction therefore exists and he tolerates it ... Or he may refuse to tolerate the contradiction; but if he does so, it is in the name of the Law of Contradiction that he does so, and refusal to tolerate the contradiction requires him to deny the validity of the Laws of Thought by which the contradiction was originally established; he has therefore no reason to refuse to tolerate the contradiction, which, if the Laws of Thought are invalid, is inoffensive. He therefore does not deny the validity of the Laws of Thought, though the contradiction is offensive and he refuses to tolerate it; or he neither tolerates the contradiction nor refuses to tolerate it, in which case he violates the Law of the Excluded middle. There is indeed a problem!

How is it dealt with? 1) The rationalist, refusing to look at his premises binds himself to the standing violation of the Laws of Thought, namely *his own existence.* 2) The mystic endorses the standing violation of the Laws by asserting their invalidity. He says, there is a mode of thinking to be developed based on the three Laws—'A is not A'; 'A is both B and not B'; 'A is neither B nor not B'. 3) The existentialist says that contradiction is the truth and I don't like it. But I can see no way out of it. Since to maintain this equivocal attitude for a long time is difficult, he either becomes a mystic or a rationalist! Of these three attitudes, the first two evade the problem by denying the Laws of Thought upon which it depends. Only the third attitude asserts the existence of the problem. Though the *puthujjana* does not see the solution of the problem, he ought to at least see that *to evade the problem is not to solve it*. He therefore chooses to endure the discomfort of the third attitude until help comes along in the Buddha's Teaching, or he himself finds the way out by becoming a Buddha. [Composed from the writings of Nanavira Thera.]

Notes

1. It can be understood to mean 'Everything is what it is' but Bradley, in *Principles of Logic*, p.141 says that in this form it is a tautology. Identity without a difference is nothing. 'It takes two to make the same, and the least we can have is some change of event in a self-same thing, or the return to that thing from some suggested difference. For, otherwise, to say, "it is the same itself" is meaningless'. Stebbing says that 'the formula may be interpreted as expressing the permanence of substance, or the persisting of something through change'. Acceptance of this principle means rejection of the popular notion that 'impermanence' in the Dhamma means 'universal flux'. With the rejection of this notion we realise that *anatta* is not about self-identity but only with 'self' as subject, 'I', 'myself', 'mine' [Adapted from Nanavira Thera.]

Chapter Thirteen
Why did the Buddha Teach?

The composition below is made from putting together the Dhamma as found in the Suttas and related texts. They are selected and arranged to stream and flow, but against the current, as presented in a thousand ways, depending on the many events in the life of the Buddha. But in everything, there is unity—coherence, consistence and connectivity. Look for this when learning the Dhamma:

Bhikkhus, both formerly and now, what I teach is dukkha and the cessation of dukkha. Be my heirs in Dhamma, not my heirs in material things. I shall teach you the Dhamma that is good in the beginning, good in the middle and good in the end, with the right meaning and phrasing; I shall reveal a holy life that is utterly perfect and pure. Let a wise man come, one who is honest and sincere, a man of rectitude. I instruct him, I teach him the Dhamma in such a way that by practising as instructed he will soon know for himself: Thus indeed there rightly comes to be liberation from the bond, that is, from the bond of ignorance. Do not be satisfied with hearsay, tradition, legendary lore, what is in the scriptures, conjecture, logical inference, weighing evidence, for a view after pondering, someone else's ability, the thought that 'the monk is our teacher'. Accept when you know *in yourself*: these ideas are wholesome, blameless, are commended by the wise, adopted and put into effect and has led to welfare and happiness. For this the Dhamma, Vaccha, is profound, hard to see and hard to understand, peaceful and sublime, unattainable by mere reasoning, subtle, to be experienced by the wise. Monks, there are three things not to be found in the world, a Tathagata would not arise in the world, an *arahat* fully enlightened; nor would a Teaching and Discipline proclaimed by a Tathagata shine in the world. What three? Birth, aging and death.

Vaccha, there is no householder, who without abandoning the fetter of householdership, on the dissolution of the body, has made an end of dukkha. This body is subject to impermanence, to being worn and rubbed away, to dissolution and disintegration. It should be regarded as impermanent, as dukkha, as a disease, as a tumor, as a dart, as a calamity, as an affliction, as alien, as disintegrating, as void, as not self. Longevity is not acquired with wealth. Nor can prosperity banish old age. Short is this life, as all the sages say, eternity it knows not, only change. As fruits fall from a tree, so too people both young and old fall when this body breaks up.

Cunda, that one who himself is sinking in the mud should pull out another who is sinking in the mud is impossible. That one who himself is not sinking in the mud should pull out another who is sinking in the mud is possible. This body is not yours or another's but is past action determined and chosen that must be experienced to be seen. What is form? The four great entities and any form derived upon them by holding are called form. Whatever matter, monks, be it past, present or future, internal or external, gross or fine, inferior or superior, far or near, is with cankers, has to do with holding—that is called the holding aggregate of matter. We are one, monks, to declare thus: Apart from matter, apart from feelings, apart from perception, apart from determinations, I will show the coming, or the going, or the disappearance, or the appearance, or the growth, or the increase, or the abundance of consciousness—that is not possible.

Usually, the world is shackled by bias, clinging and insistence. Usually, Kaccayana, this world depends upon the duality of existence and non-existence. In the world I see this generation racked by craving for being, wretched men gibbering in the face of Death, still craving, hoping for some kind of being. See how they tremble over what they claim as 'mine'—like fishes in the puddles of a failing stream.

I teach the Dhamma to one who feels. Whatever is felt counts as dukkha. But that was said by me referring to the impermanence of determinations. Here, Aggivessana, pleasant feeling arises in an untaught ordinary person. Touched by that pleasant feeling, he lusts after pleasure and continues to lust after pleasure. With the cessation of the pleasant feeling, painful feeling arises. Touched by that painful feeling, he sorrows, grieves, and laments, he weeps beating his breast and becomes distraught. When that pleasant feeling has arisen in him, it invades the mind and remains because the body is not developed. When that painful feeling has arisen in him, it invades his mind and remains because mind is not developed. Anyone in whom, in this double manner, arisen pleasant feeling invades his mind and remains because body is not developed, and arisen painful feeling invades his mind and remains because mind is not developed, is thus undeveloped in body and undeveloped in mind.

Whatever is conditioned and volitionally produced is impermanent, subject to cessation. And these five aggregates affected by holding are dependently arisen. Desire, indulgence, inclination and holding based on these five aggregates affected by holding is the origin of dukkha. The four great elements, bhikkhu, are the cause and condition for the manifestation of the material form aggregate. Contact is the cause and condition for the manifestation of the feeling aggregate ... perception aggregate ... determinations aggregate. Name and matter is the cause and condition for the manifestation of the consciousness aggregate. This world is tormented being exposed to contact. Contacted, monks, one feels, contacted one intends, contacted one perceives.

Householder, you should train thus: I will not cling to what is seen, heard, sensed, cognised, encountered, sought after and examined by the mind, and my consciousness will not be dependent on that. What does that consciousness cognise? It cognises, for example, sour, bitter, pungent, sweet, alkaline, unalkaline, salty and unsalty. It cognises that there is pleasure, that there is pain, that there is neither-pain-nor-pleasure. Consciousness is reckoned by the particular condition dependent upon which it arises—just as fire is reckoned by the particular condition depending upon which it burns. Pleasant feeling is pleasant in virtue of presence and painful in virtue of change. Painful feeling is painful in virtue of presence and pleasant in virtue of change. Neither-painful-nor-pleasant feeling is pleasant in virtue of knowledge and painful in virtue of want of knowledge.

Wrong view is the most blameworthy of all things. Now, Udayin, the pleasure and joy that arise dependent on these five cords of sensual pleasure ... should not be pursued, should not be developed, should not be cultivated, should be feared. That those recluses and brahmins who do not understand as it actually is, the gratification as gratification, the danger as danger, and the escape as escape in the case of sensual pleasure, can either themselves fully understand sensual pleasures or instruct another so that he can fully understand sensual pleasure—that is impossible. With the arising of delight, Punna, there is the arising of dukkha, I say. The evil herein is greed and hate; anger and revenge; deceit and fraud; obstinacy and presumption; conceit and arrogance; vanity and negligence.

Dependent upon *tanha*, gain; dependent upon gain, anticipation; dependent upon anticipation, attachment; dependent upon attachment, possession; dependent upon possession, jealousy; dependent upon jealousy, guarding; because of guarding, taking up clubs and knives, fights, disputes, quarrels, contention, slander, lying, and various unprofitable things come to be.

Actions make the world go round. Action makes this generation turn. Living beings are bound by action, like the chariot wheel by the pin. Student, beings are owners of their actions. They originate from their actions, are bound to their actions, have actions as their refuge. It is action that distinguishes beings as inferior or superior. That desire, that lust, that delight, that craving, that engaging and holding, that mental resolving, adherence and tendency—that is called the 'lead to being'—like a bunch of mangoes hanging from a stalk.

Determinations are impermanent. Their very nature is to rise and fall. And when there is none that arises one must cease. True bliss lies in their stilling. Bhikkhus, whatever a bhikkhu frequently thinks and ponders upon, that will become the inclination of his mind ... but with excessive thinking and pondering you will tire the body. And when the body is tired, the mind becomes strained. And when the mind is strained, it is far from concentration ... So steady the mind internally, quiet it, bring it into singleness and concentrated.

To protect oneself, bhikkhus, the foundation of mindfulness should be cultivated. To protect another, the foundation of mindfulness should be cultivated. One who protects himself protects another; one who protects another protects himself. And how, bhikkhus, does one who protects himself protect another? By cultivation, development and repeated practice. And how, bhikkhus, does one who protects another protect himself. By patience, harmlessness, kindness and forbearance.

There is a delight apart from sensual pleasures, apart from unwholesome states, which surpass divine bliss. Seclusion is happiness to one contented, who has learnt and seen the Dhamma. Friendliness towards the world is happiness to one who is forbearing of living beings. Disinterest in the world is happiness for one who has surmounted sense desires. To be rid of the conceit 'I am'—that is the greatest happiness of all.

What arises is only arising of dukkha. And what ceases is only ceasing of dukkha. In this his knowledge is independent of others. Therefore, Ananda, train thus: We will live in the way of the Dhamma, entering upon the proper way and walking in the Dhamma. To practise Dhamma is to think Dhamma, not non-Dhamma.

Chapter Fourteen

Words of Wisdom

The Buddha taught the Dhamma, presenting it as the occasion indicated, in diverse ways. There is an interesting incident recorded in the *Majjhima Nikaya*, the Middle Length Discourses of the Buddha. The king's carpenter, Pancakanga, frequently met the Buddha and senior disciples to learn and discuss Dhamma. One day, he met the Venerable Udayin and said, "Venerable sir, how many kinds of feeling have been stated by the Blessed One?" "Three kinds of feeling have been stated by the Blessed One," replied Venerable Udayin firmly. "Not three kinds, sir, but two kinds," countered Pancakanga. A discussion followed but the carpenter insisted he was correct. Venerable Ananda heard of the incident and informed the Buddha. "Ananda, it was actually a true presentation that the carpenter Pancakanga would not accept from Udayin, and it was actually a true presentation that Udayin would not accept from the carpenter Pancakanga … When the Dhamma has thus been shown by me in presentations, it may be expected of those who will not concede, allow, and accept what is well stated and well spoken by others that they will take to quarrelling …" [Paraphrased]

But throughout his description and exposition of the Dhamma, there ran a constant theme, the rubric of the Dhamma: *N' etam mama, n' esoham asmi, n' eso me atta'* [Not, this is mine; not, this am I; not, this is my self.] In a potter's shed one night, he told the monk Pukkusati, 'The tides of conceiving do not sweep over one who stands upon and has not neglected wisdom, preserved truth, cultivated relinquishment and trained for peace; and when the tides of conceiving no longer sweep over him he is called a sage at peace'. [Adapted from M 140]

The Buddha said he is 'Thus gone,' is untraceable here and now and cannot be reckoned in terms of [*puthujjana*] consciousness.

The following quotations seek to guide the reader to make personal effort to understand the Dhamma in any one or more of its facets. Ponder on the words of wisdom of the Buddha and disciples. They are not arranged in any particular order.

Words of Wisdom

- Friends, the Blessed One describes pleasure not only with reference to pleasant feeling; rather, friends, the Tatagatha describes pleasure as any kind of pleasure wherever and in whatever way it is found.
- 'But what herein is pleasant Venerable Sariputta, since herein [Nibbana] there is nothing felt?' 'Just this is pleasant, friend, that herein there is nothing felt'. [Sariputta]

- Though some may count extremes, they find no essence but renew their bonds; for they dwell in the seen and the sensed— like moths that fall into a flame.

- What goes against the stream [*patisotagami*] is subtle, deep and hard to see, abstruse.

- Bhikkhus, it is with ordered attention [*manasikara*], with ordered effort that I have reached and have realised the supreme deliverance.

- It [the Middle Way] gives vision, gives knowledge, and leads to peace; to direct knowledge, to enlightenment, to Nibbana.

- Just as in a peaked house, monks, all are joined at the peak, all are destroyed with the destruction of the peak, even so, monks, whatever unskilled things there are, all are converged in nescience, all are joined in nescience, all are destroyed with the destruction of nescience.

- A bhikkhu, whose heart is liberated sides with none, disputes with none and he employs, though without misapprehension, the speech current in the world.

- A man's virtue is to be known by living with him, and then only if we attend not a little over a long period, if we neither fail in attention, nor lack understanding. A man's purity is to be known by talking with him. A man's fortitude is to be known in times of adversity. A man's understanding is to be known by discussing with him.

- Living alone is perfected thus: the past is left behind, the future is renounced and lust and desire for the selfhood acquired in the present is put away.

- Just as a yellow leaf fallen from its stalk is incapable of becoming green again, so too, Sunnakkhatta, when a person is intent on the imperturbable, he has shed the fetter of worldly material things.

- Just as a bird, wherever it goes, flies with its wings as its only burden, so too, the bhikkhu becomes content with robes to protect his body and lives with almsfood to maintain his stomach, and wherever he goes, he sets out taking only these with him.

- The acrobat Uggasena standing perilously balanced on the top of a bamboo pole performing risky acrobatics heard the Buddha say: 'Let go in front; let go behind; let go in the middle'.

- Just as the flight path of birds in the air is untraceable, the track of the *arahat* is not found.

- With the arising of delight (*nandi*), Punna, there is the arising of suffering, I say.

- Just as the footprint of any living being that walks can be placed within an elephant's footprint, all skillful states can be included in the Four Nobel Truths. [Sariputta]

- So I have shown you how the Dhamma is similar to a raft, being for the purpose of crossing over, not for the purpose of grasping.

- The following, Gotami, do **not** lead to Dhamma: passion, not dispassion; attachment, not detachment; amassing, not dispersal; ambition, not modesty; discontentment, not contentment; association, not seclusion; idleness, not energy; luxury, not frugality. [Discourse to his foster mother Mahapajapati.]

- A stupid/intelligent man, monks, has thus acquired this body. So there is just this body and name and matter externally. In that way there is a dyad.

- Perception, Pottapada, arises first, knowledge afterwards; but with the arising of perception there is arising of knowledge.

- And what, monks, is perception? It is these six bodies of perception, namely: sight-perception, sound-perception, smell-perception, taste-perception, touch-perception, idea-perception. This is called perception.

- Seven qualities of a *kalyanamitra* [true friend] are: He inspires love, inspires respect, inspires emulation, is a counselor, is a patient listener, is able to deliver deep discourses or treat profound subjects and never leads one in harmful or useless pursuits.

- Imperfections that defile the mind are: covetousness, unrighteous greed, ill will, anger, revenge, contempt, domineering attitude, envy, avarice, deceit, fraud, obstinacy, presumption, conceit, arrogance, vanity. [These defilements are abolished in the following stages: 1. *Sotapatti* or path of stream entry—contempt, domineering attitude, envy, avarice, deceit, fraud. 2. *Anagami* or path of non-returning— ill will, anger, revenge, negligence. 3. Arahant—covetousness and unrighteous greed, obstinacy, presumption, conceit, arrogance, vanity.]

- Five factors of striving: 1. Has faith in the Buddha. 2. Is free from illness and affliction, possessing a good digestion. 3. Is honest and sincere. 4. Is energetic. 5. Has wisdom.

- Five things that may turn out to be true or false are : 1. Faith. 2. Approval. 3. Oral tradition. 4. Reasoned cogitation. 5. Reflective acceptance of a view.

- Requirements for final arrival at truth: striving, scrutiny, application of will, zeal, reflective acceptance of teaching, examination of the meaning, memorising the teaching, hearing the Dhamma, giving ear to the teacher, paying respect to the teacher, visiting the teacher, having faith in the teacher.

- Four kinds of striving: 1. Awakens zeal for non-arising of unarisen evil states. 2. Awakens zeal for abandoning of arisen evil states. 3. Awakens zeal for arising of non-arisen good states. 4. Awakens zeal for continuation of arisen good states.

- Just as anyone who has extended his mind over the great ocean has included within it whatever streams there are that flow into the ocean; so too, anyone who has developed and cultivated mindfulness of the body has included within himself whatever wholesome states there are that partake of true knowledge.

- Five courses of speech others may address you: timely or untimely; true or untrue; gentle or harsh; connected with good or connected with harm; with *metta* or with inner hate.

- Five ways of removing distracting thoughts. 1. Give attention to some other sign connected with wholesome thoughts. 2. Examine the danger of unwholesome thoughts. 3. Try to forget the unwholesome thoughts and give no attention. 4. Give attention to stilling the evil thought determination. 5. Beat down, constrain and crush the mind.

- In whom, monks, altogether and in every way, there are not these five faculties [*indriya*], of him I say 'An Outsider', one who stands on the commoner's side.

- This body is not yours, nor another's but is past action (already) determined and chosen that must be experienced to be seen.

- The wise man, having got beyond conceiving, might say 'I say'; and he might say, 'They said to me'. Skilled in worldly expressions, knowing about them, he might use them within the limits of usage.

- But, Udayi, let be the past, let be the future, I shall set you forth the Teaching: When there is this this is, with arising of this this arises; when there is not this this is not, with the cessation of this this ceases.

- Then, Bahiya, you should train yourself thus: 'In the seen there shall be just the seen; in the heard there shall be just the heard; in the sensed there shall be just the sensed; in the cognised there shall be just the cognised'—Thus, Bahiya you should train yourself. When, Bahiya, for you, in the seen there shall be just the seen ... cognised, then, Bahiya, you (will) not (be) that by which (tvam na tena); when, Bahiya, you (shall) not (be) that by which, then, Bahiya, you (shall) not (be) in that place (tvam na tattha); When, Bahiya, you (shall) not (be) in that place, then, Bahiya, you (will) neither (be) here nor yonder nor between the two. Just this is the end of *dukkha*. [Udana 1.10]

Selections from the Dhammapada

The Dhammapada are a collection of 423 statements of the Buddha uttered by him on about 300 different occasions. They are in euphonic beautiful often-rhythmic Pali verse form and have been translated into several languages. I have selected and paraphrased some verses to bring out the elegance and timeless profundity of the speech of the Buddha, and the unforgettable similes used extempore. (Refer to the original from the verse number given.)

1. Mind is foremost. Everything is mind-made. Mind is the forerunner of states. If one speak or act with a wicked mind, *dukkha* shall follow just as the wheel the hoof of the draught-ox. [No 001]

2. Mind is foremost. Everything is mind-made. Mind is the forerunner of states. If one speak or act with a pure mind, happiness follows just as the shadow that never leaves. [No 002]

3. In this world, hatreds never cease through hatred. Through love alone do they cease. This is an eternal law. [No 005]

4. Even as rain penetrates an ill-thatched house, so lust penetrates an undeveloped mind. Even as rain does not penetrate a well-thatched house, so lust does not penetrate a well-developed mind. [Nos 013, 014]

5. Diligence is the path to the 'deathless', and heedlessness the path to death. The diligent do not die. The heedless are like the dead. [No 021]

6. The flitting fickle mind is difficult to guard and difficult to control. Just as the fletcher straightens his arrow, the wise straightens the mind. [No 033]

7. As a fish taken out from water and thrown upon the land flutters, so does this mind therein with passions not abandoned. [No 034]

8. Alas! This body will lie on the ground, cast away, bereft of consciousness—just as a rotten useless log of wood. [No 041]

9. A sage should go about the village as a bee collects honey and flies away without harming the flower. [No 049]

10. Just as a beautiful flower without scent is of no value so also is the well-spoken word of one who does not practise. [No 052]

11. Just as a garland is made from a collection of flowers, this mortal man should do many good deeds. [No 053]

12. If as a disciple, he journeys and meets no companion better than he or equal, even so, let there be no fellowship with a fool. [No 061]

13. Thus do fools exclaim: I have sons! I have wealth! In truth, he himself is not his own. So what for sons, what for wealth? [No 062]

14. The fool who knows he is a fool—for that very reason is not a fool. A fool indeed is a fool who thinks he is wise. [No 63]

15. Though throughout his life a fool may associate with the wise, he no more shall understand the Dhamma as a spoon tastes the flavour of soup. [No 064]

16. Just as the tongue quickly tastes the flavour of soup, the intelligent understand Dhamma even when with the wise but a moment. [No 065]

17. An evil deed is sweet as honey so does a fool think, until it ripens in grief. [No 069]

18. Just as milk curdle not instantly, an evil deed does not bear fruit at once. It follows the fool like smoldering fire covered with ash. [No 071]

19. Irrigators lead water. Fletchers straighten shafts. Carpenters bend wood. The wise controls them. [No 080]

20. Just as a solid rock is not shaken by wind, the wise are not disturbed either by praise or by blame. [No 081]

21. Few among men are there who go Beyond. The rest run about on the shore. [No 085]

22. One who subdues the five senses like steeds well-trained by a charioteer, whose pride is overcome and is free from corruption, that one even the Gods hold dear. [No 094]

23. Do not disregard evil, thinking 'It shall not come upon me'. Falling raindrops fill even a water jar. A fool likewise collects little by little, until filled with evil. [No 121]

24. Just as poison does not affect one with no wound on the hand and one may carry it, no harm shall affect a person who does no wrong. [No 124]

25. When you silence yourself like a cracked gong, you have already attained Nibbana as no vindictiveness is in you. [No 134]

26. A man of little learning grows old like the ox. Though his muscles grow, his wisdom grows not. [No 152]

27. Oneself alone does evil. It is self-born and self-conditioned. Evil grinds the unwise just as diamond a gem. [No 161]

28. It is easy to do things that are hard but not beneficial. It is very difficult to do things beneficial and good. [No 163]

29. Do not neglect one's welfare for the sake of others, however great. Seeing clearly one's own welfare be intent on one's own goal. [No 166]

30. To do no evil, to cultivate good, to purify the mind—this is the teaching of the Buddhas. [No 182]

31. Victory breeds hatred. The defeated live in pain. Giving up victory and defeat, the wise live in peace. [No 201]

32. There is no fire like lust and no crime like hate and no sickness like this body. There is no bliss higher than Peace. [No 202]

33. The greatest disease is hunger. The five aggregates of holding are the greatest sickness. Knowing this as it actually is, Nibbana is supreme bliss. [No 203]

34. Mental health is the highest wealth and contentment the greatest gain. The trustworthy are the best kinsmen. Nibbana is the highest bliss. [No 204]

35. Do not associate with those that are dear and never with those not dear, for it is painful not to see the dear and painful to see those not dear. [No 210]

36. From endearment is born grief, from endearment is born fear. Set free from endearment, there is no grief, nor fear. [No 212]

37. From love is born grief. From love is born fear. Set free from love, there is no grief, nor fear. [No 213]

38. From attachment is born grief. From attachment is born fear. Set free from attachment, there is no grief, nor fear. [No 214]

39. From lust is born grief. From lust is born fear. Set free from lust, there is no grief, nor fear. [No 215]

40. From craving is born grief. From craving is born fear. Set free from craving, there is no grief, nor fear. [No 216]

41. Overcome anger with love. Overcome evil with good. Overcome being miserly by giving. Vanquish the liar with truth. [No 223]

42. Atula, this is an old saying, not one said only in these climes: 'They blame those who are silent and also they who speak too much; and blame even those who speak little'. There is no one that is not blamed in this world. [No 227]

43. There never was, never shall be nor does exist a person wholly blamed or wholly praised. [No 227]

44. Just as rust in iron eats its way when it comes to be, by one's own deeds is the transgressor led to states of woe. [No 240]

45. There is no fire like lust, no obsession like hate, no trap like delusion and no river like craving. [No 251]

46. Easily seen are the faults of others. It is hard to see your own. Like the chaff, one winnows the faults of others. As a poultry-thief conceals him, one hides one's own by deceit. [No 252]

47. In the sky lie no tracks. The sage leaves no external trace. While mankind delights in inference and adherence, the Tathagatha is freed from all. [No 254]

48. The effort you must make yourself. Tathagathas only point the way. [No 276]

49. All conditioned things are impermanent. When one sees this with wisdom, one is wearied of *dukkha*. This is the path to liberation. [No 277]

50. All conditioned things are *dukkha*. When one sees this with wisdom, one is wearied of *dukkha*. This is the path to liberation. [No 278]

51. All conditioned things are not self. When one sees this with wisdom, one is wearied of *dukkha*. This is the path to liberation. [No 279]

52. No sons, neither father nor kinsmen can save you. Doomed to die, there is no protection for anyone among kinsmen. [No 288]

53. It is better to swallow a red-hot iron ball from flaming fire than be immoral and uncontrolled while feeding on alms offered by people. [No 308]

54. The stupid one, sluggish, gluttonous and sleepy, wallowing like a great big pig fed on hogwash—goes from rebirth to rebirth. [No 325]

55. Just as a tree cut down, with roots unharmed and virile, sprouts again, when dormant craving is not uprooted, *dukkha* shall arise again and again. [No 338]

56. Let go in front. Let go behind. Let go in the middle. Cross to the farther shore. Released from everything, do not undergo birth and decay again. [No 348]

57. The gift of the Dhamma excels all gifts. The taste of the Dhamma excels all taste. The pleasure of the Dhamma excels all pleasure. He who has destroyed craving has overcome all *dukkha*. [No 354]

58. Just as weeds are the bane of fields, lust is the bane of mankind. What is given to those freed from lust shall bear abundance of fruit. [No 356]

59. Just as weeds are the bane of fields, hatred is the bane of mankind. What is given to those freed from hatred shall bear abundance of fruit. [No 357]

60. Just as weeds are the bane of fields, delusion is the bane of mankind. What is given to those freed from delusion lust shall bear abundance of fruit. [No 358]

61. Just as weeds are the bane of fields, craving is the bane of mankind. What is given to those freed from craving shall bear abundance of fruit. [No 359]

62. He that utters gentle, instructive true words and gives offence to no one—him I call a brahmin. [No 408]

63. He who has no likes and dislikes, is cooled and undefiled, has conquered the world and is diligent—him I call a brahmin. [No 418]

64. He who does not hold to that which is past, future and present, and is without holding to anything—him I call a brahmin. [No 421]

Chapter Fifteen
Just Let It Be

A condensation of the discourses of Achaan Chah from the book 'A Still Forest Pool' with kind permission from its editor meditation master Jack Kornfield

Let us talk about the difference between studying the Dhamma and applying them in practice. True Dhamma study has only one purpose— to find a way out of the unsatisfactoriness of our lives. Our suffering has causes for its arising and a place to abide. Therefore the Buddha taught us to contemplate the movements of the mind. Watching the mind move, we can see its basic characteristics: endless change, unsatisfactoriness, and emptiness.

The Buddha did not want us to become attached to words. He just wanted us to *see* that all is impermanent, unsatisfactory, empty of self. He taught only to let go. Just let them be, the good as well as the bad. The Buddha said simply, "Give them up". But for us, it is necessary to study our own minds to know how it is possible to give them up. We can discover this through meditation. Meditation is like a single log of wood. Insight and investigation are at one end of the log; calm and concentration are at the other end. If you lift up the whole log, both sides come up at once. Which is concentration and which is insight? Just this mind. Such terms are only conventions for teaching.

We should not be attached to the language. *The only source of true knowledge is to see what is within us.* Therefore, develop *samadhi* and *vipassana*, calm and insight; learn to make them arise in your mind and really use them. Otherwise, you will know only the words of Buddhism. But repeated practice is crucial. If someone curses us and we have no feelings of self, the incident ends with the spoken words, and we do not suffer. *If we do not stand in the line of fire, we do not get shot.*

Move gracefully through the world not caught in evaluating each event, not discriminating, not thinking *what it should be.* Be aware of things *just as they are.* Do not put a mental construction on them. You will be a different person. Why not try it?

Many people who have studied on a university level and attained graduate degrees and worldly success find their lives are still lacking. *The vulture flies high, but what does it feed on?*

Dhamma is understanding that goes beyond the conditioned, compounded, limited understanding of worldly science. It is necessary to teach the basics first—basic morality, seeing the transitoriness of life, the facts of aging and death. Of course, the Dhamma books are correct, *but they are not right. They cannot give you right understanding.* To see the word *hatred* in print is not the same as experiencing anger. Only experiencing for yourself can give you true faith.

There are two kinds of faith. One is a kind of blind trust in the Buddha, in the teachings, in the master, which often leads one to begin practice or to ordain. The second is true faith—certain, unshakable— which arises from knowing oneself. To attain this certainty in one's practice, you must go beyond all words, all symbols, all plans for your practice. *If you do not turn inward, you will never know reality.*

Do not hold on to anything. *Just observe things as they are.* You need not study much. You will see the Dhamma for yourself. Observe your own mind. If you cut off this verbal, thinking mind, you will have a true standard for judging. Practise in this way and the rest will follow.

The true Eightfold Path is within us—two eyes, two ears, two nostrils, a tongue and a body. These eight doors are our entire Path and the mind is the one that walks on the Path. Know these doors, examine them, and all the *dhammas* will be revealed. No need for long explanations.

Give up clinging to love and hate, *just rest with things as they are.* That is all I do in my own practice. Do not try to become anything. Do not make yourself into anything. Do not be a meditator. Do not become enlightened. When you sit, let it be. When you walk, let it be. Grasp at nothing. Resist nothing. There are dozens of meditation techniques to develop *samadhi* and many kinds of *vipassana*. But it all comes back to this—*just let it all be.*

You will see that when the heart/mind is unattached, it is abiding in its *normal* state. When it stirs from the normal because of various thoughts and feelings, the process of thought construction takes place, in which illusions are created. Learn to see through this process. Good or bad only arises in your mind. If you keep a watch on your mind, studying this one topic your whole life, I guarantee you will never be bored.

For the most part, our thinking follows sense objects, and wherever our thoughts lead us, we follow. However, thinking and wisdom are different. *In wisdom, the mind becomes still*, unmoving, and we are simply aware, simply acknowledging. Normally, when sense objects come, we think about, dwell on and worry. Yet none of those sense objects is substantial. All are impermanent, unsatisfactory.

Mind is one thing, the one who knows is another. When you make contact with sense objects, contemplate: impermanent, unsatisfactory, not self. File everything under these three categories, and keep contemplating. Everywhere you look is the Dhamma. There is nothing in the world that is not Dhamma. But you must understand. Happiness and unhappiness, pleasure and pain are always with us. *If you don't relate to phenomena as being you* or see yourself as their owner, the mind comes into balance. This balance is the correct path, the correct teaching of the Buddha that leads to liberation, non-grasping or *vimukti*. When you understand this balance, then the path becomes clear.

Everything is like an old banana peel or a coconut husk—you have no use for it, no fascination with it. When you see that things in the world are like banana peels, then you are free to walk in the world without being bothered or hurt in any way. This is the path that brings you to freedom.

The very desire to be free or to be enlightened will be the desire that prevents your freedom. You can try hard as you wish, practise ardently night and day, *but if you still have the desire to achieve, you will never find the peace*. The energy from this desire will cause doubt and restlessness. No matter how long and hard you practise, wisdom will not arise from desire. *Simply let go.*

The practice is to sit and let your heart become still and concentrated and then to use that concentration to examine the nature of the mind and body. Otherwise, if you simply make the heart/mind quiet, it will be peaceful and free of defilement only as long as you sit. This is like using a stone to cover a garbage pit; when you take away the stone, the pit is still infested and full of garbage.

Examining the mind and body most directly does not involve the use of thought. There are two levels of examination. One is thoughtful and discursive. The other is a silent, concentrated, *inner listening*. Only when the heart is concentrated and still, can real wisdom naturally arise. It is this *seeing* that leads you to learn about change, about emptiness, and about the selflessness of body and mind.

The Buddha talked about two styles of practice: liberation through wisdom and liberation through concentration. People whose style is liberation through wisdom hear the Dhamma and immediately begin to understand it. Since the entire teaching is simply to let go of things, to let things be, they begin the practice of letting go in a very natural way, without a great deal of effort or concentration.

The Dhamma of the Buddha is not found in books. Just be mindful of whatever there is to see. This is the way to the truths of the Buddha. Everything you do in your life is a chance to practise. It is all Dhamma.

The Dhamma belongs to no one; it has no owner. It arises in the world when the world manifests, yet stands alone as the truth. It is always here, unmoving, limitless, for all who seek it. It is like water underground—*whoever digs a well finds it.* Yet *whether or not you dig, it is always here, underlying all things.* Truth is hidden in untruth, permanence in impermanence.

To understand 'not self', you have to meditate. If you only intellectualise, your head will explode. When you see beyond self, you no longer cling to happiness, and *when you no longer cling to happiness, you can begin to be truly happy.*

Our discrimination colours everything. This is the world we create. Two persons are watching a flag: one says it is the wind that moves, the other says it is the flag. They can argue for ever. For it is the mind that moves. Why is sugar sweet and water tasteless? It is just their nature. So too with thinking and stillness, pain and pleasure. Ultimately, things are just as they are—*only comparisons cause us to suffer.* It is like a monkey jumping senselessly. Its behaviour is driven not by dispassion but by different forms of aversion and fear.

You have to learn to control. We can see the mind as a lotus. Some lotuses are still stuck in the mud, some have climbed above the mud but are still under water, some have reached the surface, while others are open in the sun, stainfree. Which lotus do you choose to be?

Whether the fruit of wisdom comes quickly or slowly, you cannot force it, just as you cannot force the growth of a tree you have planted. If the mind does not know what it needs to do, it will try to force the plant to grow and flower and give fruit in one day. Just practise in the right direction and leave the rest to your *karma.* Proper effort is not the effort to make something particular happen. It is the effort to be *aware and awake in each moment,* the effort to overcome laziness and defilement, the effort to make each activity of our day meditation.

Right effort and virtue are not a question of what you do outwardly but to constant inner awareness and restraint. Do not be attached to big and small, important and unimportant.

Constantly watch over your mind as a parent watches over a child. You must constantly make the effort to know yourself. It is necessary as your breathing, which continues in all situations. Rely on yourself. Do not find fault with others. If they behave wrongly, there is no need for you to suffer. If I take poison, there is no need for you to suffer.

Real love is wisdom. What most people think of as love is just an impermanent feeling. If you have a nice taste every day, you will soon get tired of it. We cannot suppress nor forbid such feelings. We just should not cling to or identify with them but should know them for what they are.

Boredom is a real problem. If we look closely we can see that the mind is always active. Conceptual thinking creates illusion and embellishment beyond the simple truth here in front of you. Do everything with a mind that lets go.

Doubting is natural. Everyone starts with doubts. You can learn a great deal from them. What is important is that you don't identify with your doubts. That is, don't get caught up in them, letting your mind spin in endless circles. Instead, watch the whole process of doubting, of wondering. See who it is that doubts. See how doubts come and go. Just let go of what you are attached to. Let go of your doubts and simply watch. This is how one can end doubting.

There is one essential point that all good practice must come eventually come to—*not clinging.* In the end, *you must let go of all meditation systems.* Let go of your opinions and watch yourself. If you are annoyed, watch the annoyance in your own mind. Just be mindful of your own actions; simply examine yourself and your feelings. Then you will understand. This is the way to practice.

Just try to keep your mind in the present. Whatever arises in the mind, just watch it and let go of it. Don't even wish to be rid of thoughts. Avoid discrimination between good and bad, hot and cold, fast and slow.

If doubts arise, watch them come and go. It is very simple. Hold on to nothing. It is as though you are walking down a road. Periodically you will run into obstacles. When you meet defilements, just see them and overcome them by letting them go. Don't think about the obstacles you've already passed; don't worry about those you have not yet seen. Stick to the present. Everything is changing. Whatever you pass, don't cling to it. Eventually the mind will reach its natural balance where practice is automatic. *All things will come and go of themselves.*

You must get rid of your cleverness. A cup filled with dirty, stale water is useless. Only after the old water is thrown out can the cup become useful. You must empty your mind of opinions; then you will see. If you think, "I am clever, I am wealthy, I am important, I understand all about Buddhism," you cover up the truth of *anatta*, or non-self. All you see is self, I, and mine. But Buddhism is letting go of self— voidness, emptiness, *Nibbana*. If you think yourself better than others, you will only suffer.

Body, speech and mind all make *karma* when we cling to them. We create habits that can make us suffer in future. All things are conditioned by cause. But you need not bother to think about past, present, or future; merely watch the body and mind now. Don't cling to or watch others.

When you have seen the truth you are freed from views and opinions. Everything becomes peaceful but peace too must be seen as impermanent. If you are attached to peaceful states of mind, you will suffer when you do not have them. Give up everything, even peace.

To teach other people is a beautiful and important responsibility that one should accept with a full heart. The way to do it properly is to understand that in teaching others you must always be teaching yourself. You have to take care of your own practice and your own purity. It's not enough to simply tell others what's correct.

Acknowledge what is pure and what is not. The essence of the Buddha's teaching is to learn to see things truthfully, fully and clearly. Seeing the truth in itself brings freedom.

You must examine yourself. Know who you are. Know your body and mind by simply watching. In sitting, in sleeping, in eating, know your limits. The practice is not to achieve anything. Just be mindful of what is. Don't practise too strictly. Don't get caught up with outward form. Simply be natural and watch.

Don't discriminate. Would you be upset at a small tree in the forest for not being tall and straight like some others? Don't judge other people. No need to carry the burden of wishing to change them all. Learn the value of giving and of devotion. Practise morality; live simply and naturally; watch the mind.

There is no one here, *just this*. No owner, no one to be old, to be young, to be good or bad, weak or strong. Just this, that's all. Various elements of nature playing them out, all empty. No one born and no one to die. Use the understanding that you have already developed to persevere in practice. With the proper effort and with time, understanding will unfold by itself. But in all cases, use your own natural wisdom.

What we have spoken of is what I feel is helpful to you. If you do it, you can come to the end of all doubt. Only you can do that. *From now on it's up to you.*

Useful Pali Words

akālika	-	immediately effective, without time
abhijjā	-	covetousness
abhiññā	-	direct knowledge
abhisaṅkaroti	-	to generate, to perform
abhisaṅkhāta	-	conditioned
abyapāda	-	non ill will
acinteyya	-	not to be speculated about, unthinkable
adinnādānā	-	taking what is not given
adivacana	-	designation
ahankāra	-	I-making
akālika	-	taking no time
akāsa	-	space
akusala	-	unwholesome, unskillful
anāgāmī	-	non-returner
anagāriya	-	homeless
anattā	-	'not self'
anicca	-	impermanent
aniccatā	-	impermanence
animitta	-	signless

anukampā	-	compassion
anuloma	-	with the grain [opposite of patiloma]
anupādisesa	-	without residue
appamāda	-	diligence
arahat	-	one who is worthy, usually untranslated
arati	-	discontent
ariya	-	noble
ariyasacca	-	noble truth
ariyasāvaka	-	noble disciple
arūpa	-	immaterial
asaṅkhata	-	unconditioned
asekha	-	one gone beyond training, the arahat
asmimāna	-	not self; conceit 'I am'
assāda	-	gratification
assāsapassāsā	-	in and out breaths
asubha	-	foul
asutavā	-	uninstructed
atakkavācara	-	not attainable by mere reasoning or logic
atamyata	-	non-identification
attavāda	-	belief in a self
attā	-	self
aṭṭhapuarisapuggalā	-	the eight individuals
avihimsā	-	non-cruelty
avijjā	-	ignorance, non-knowledge of the four noble truths
ayoniso	-	unwise
ādīnava	-	danger
āhara	-	nutriment
ājīva	-	livelihood
āmisa	-	worldly, material thing

ānapānāsati	-	mindfulness of in and out breathing
āneñja	-	imperturbable
ānidassana	-	non-indicative
āpo	-	water
āsava	-	taint
āyatana	-	base
āyu	-	life
bala	-	power
bhava	-	being, existence
bhikkhu	-	monk
bhikkhuni	-	nun
cāga	-	generosity, relinquishment
cakkhu	-	eye
cetanā	-	volition, intention, choice
cetasika	-	mental
chanda	-	zeal, desire
citta	-	mind, consciousness, cognition, purpose, experience
cittavithi	-	mental process, cognitive series
dhātu	-	element
ditthi	-	view, usually wrong view
domanassa	-	grief
ekaggatā	-	unification of mind
ekāyana	-	going in one direction
hetu	-	condition, cause
hetu pacchayā	-	
iddhi	-	feat of supernormal power
iddhipāda	-	four bases of spiritual power
indriya	-	faculty
iriyapātha	-	posture

irodha	-	cessation [Opposite is samudaya, arising]
jarā	-	aging
jāti	-	birth
jhāna	-	state of meditation
kāma	-	sensual desire
kāmacchanda	-	sensual desire
kāmasukhallikānauyoga	-	being addicted to sensual desire
kamma	-	action
karunā	-	compassion
kāya	-	body
khanda	-	aggregate
khānti	-	acceptance of view, forebearance
kusala	-	wholesome, skillful
lābha	-	gain
lakkhana	-	mark, characteristic
lobha	-	lust
loka	-	world
lokuttara	-	beyond the world, world transcending
magga	-	path
māhabhūta	-	four great entities
mama	-	mine, me
manasikāra	-	attention
mano	-	mind
maññana	-	coceiving
maññati	-	to conceive
marana	-	death
micchāditthi	-	wrong view [Opposite of sammāditthi]
moha	-	delusion
musāvadā	-	speak falsehood

nāma	-	name, designation, knowledge
nāmarūpa	-	name and matter
ñāna	-	knowledge
nekkhamma	-	renunciation, freedom from lust
nibbāna	-	extinction
niruddha	-	ceased
opanayiko	-	leading
ottapa	-	fear of wrong doing
pānatipātā	-	killing living beings
pabajjā	-	going forth
paccayā	-	condition
pañcakkhanda	-	five aggregates
pañcíupādānakkhandā	-	five aggregates with holding
paññā	-	wisdom
parinibbāna	-	final nibbana
paticcasamuppāda	-	dependent arising
paticcasamuppannā	-	dependently arisen
patiloma	-	against the grain
patisotagāmi	-	going against the stream
phala	-	fruit
pharusa vacā	-	speak harshly
phassa	-	contact
pisuna vacā	-	speak maliciously
puggala	-	individual
punabhavabhinibbāti	-	coming into renewed being
puñña	-	merit
puthajjana	-	uninstructed commoner
rāga	-	lust
rūpa	-	matter, form
sāupādisesa	-	with residue

sacca	-	truth
saddhā	-	faith, confidence, trust
sakkāya	-	person, personality
sakkāyaditthi	-	personality view
samādhi	-	concentration
sammāditthi	-	right view
sampajañña	-	awareness
samudāya	-	arising
sanditthika	-	evident, immediately visible
sangha	-	Order, Community of monks
sañjānāti	-	to perceive
sankhāra	-	determination, determinant
sankhāta	-	determined
saññā	-	perception
sati	-	mindfulness, recollection
Sāupādisesa	-	with residue
sekha	-	one in training
somanassa	-	joy
sotāpanna	-	stream-attainer
sotāptti	-	attaining of the stream
takka	-	reasoning
tanhā	-	craving
tejo	-	fire
thinna	-	sloth
thinna midda	-	sloth and torpor
tulana	-	scrutiny
udhacca	-	restlessness
upādāna	-	holding, clinging
upasampadā	-	full admission
upavicarati	-	to explore

upekkhā	-	equanimity
vāci	-	speech
vedanā	-	feeling
vicāra	-	pondering
vicikiccā	-	doubt
vijjā	-	science
vimutti	-	deliverance, liberation
viññāna	-	consciousness
vipāka	-	result, ripening
virāga	-	dispassion, fading away
viriya	-	energy, exertion
vitakka	-	thinking, pondering

Abbreviations

A - Anguttara Nikāya

D - Digha Nikāya

M - Majjhima Nikāya

Sn-Samyutta Nikāya

Dhp - Dhammapada

Recommended Books

1. Ñānavira Thera, *Writings of Ñānavira Thera, Notes on Dhamma*, vol. I, Buddhist Cultural Centre, 125, Anderson Road, Dehiwela, Sri Lanka, 2003.

2. Ñānavira Thera, *Writings of Ñānavira Thera, Letters*, vol. II, Buddhist Cultural Centre, 125, Anderson Road, Dehiwela, Sri Lanka, 2003.

3. Ñānamoli Thera, *The Life of the Buddha*, Buddhist Publication Society, Kandy, Sri Lanka, re-printed 1998.

4. Bhikkhu Ñānamoli and Bhikkhu Bodhi, *The Middle Length Discourses of the Buddha, A New Translation of the Majjhima Nikaya*, Wisdom Publications, USA, 1995 and Buddhist Publication Society, Kandy, Sri Lanka, 1995.

5. Narada Thera, *The Dhammapada*, Buddhist Cultural Centre, 125, Anderson Road, Dehiwela, Sri Lanka, 2003.

6. John D Ireland, *The Udana and The Itivuttaka*, Buddhist Publication Society, Kandy, Sri Lanka, 1997. .

7. Walpola Rahula, *The Taming of the Bull,* Godage and Sons, Maradana, Colombo, re-printed, 2003.

Annexure

VENERABLE ÑĀNAVIRA THERA (1920-65)

Harold Musson was an only child, born in army barracks in Aldershot, England in 1920. His father was a rich man owning coalmines in Wales and who commanded a battalion of the British Army in Burma where Harold spent a few years as a child of seven years. One day, he asked, "Who is the Buddha?" and when told "the Buddha was a man who sat under a tree and got enlightened", he said, "That is what I want to do!" Harold graduated from Cambridge University at the age of twenty-one years with First Class Honors in modern languages and in mathematics.

In the last World War, he served as a captain assigned to interrogate prisoners of war in Italy. In 1945, he fell ill and in his hospital bed in Sorrento, he read the book '*La Dottrina del Risveglio*' by Julius Evola a born Catholic. Evola had written that his aim was to illuminate the true nature of original Buddhism, weakened to the point of obscurity in subsequent forms whereas the essential spirit of the doctrine was determined by a will for the unconditioned, confirmed by investigation that leads to mastery over life and death. Impressed by the book, and by Evola, a well-known rebel in Italy and Germany, Harold translated it to English as the '*The Doctrine of Awakening—A Study in Buddhist Ascesis*'. [Luzac, London, 1951].

Osbert Moore was with Harold in Italy at the time. [See biography of Ñānamoli Thera]. After the War, Harold had no need to do a job. He led a Bohemian life indulging in 'wine', women and 'song', smoking forty cigarettes a day. One day, when, walking in Hyde Park one evening, he gave up smoking with grim determination. The words of the Buddha on self-discipline haunted him and he saw the futility of his mode of life as a rich playboy. So when he met his army friend Osbert at a London pub one night, they both decided to explore the Teaching of the Buddha. They arrived in Ceylon in 1948 after a brief experimentation with *yoga* in India and became pupils of the Venerable Nyanatiloka Maha Thera of the Island Hermitage, Dodanduwa, learning Pali and the Dhamma. Harold was ordained as Ñānavira and later studied under Palane Sri Vajiranana Maha Nayake Thera of Vajiraramaya as his Upajjhaya [to whom he dedicated the only book he wrote].

Ñānavira from his young days, was a person who regarded other people not as 'we' but as 'they' and inclined to solitude. He did not like curious visitors at the Hermitage, and he went to various *arannayas*. He found them a charade and found the ideal place in the Bundala Forest Reserve, thirteen miles away from Hambantota. A local *dayaka* helped him to build a zinc shed. Bundala is supposed to be the village of the washerwomen and men of King Dutugemunu. It was then a remote, poor community living in wattle and daub houses. The gravel road off the highway running in a straight line through sand and scrub and forest and lagoons where flamingos nest when it is winter in Europe ended in a fishing *wadiya*. About halfway is a culvert over a shallow perennial pond of water, and hidden by thorn brush and gnarled trees, is a narrow footpath to the *kuti* with a corridor and one room of brick and mud, built later. Here Ñānavira Thera lived, strived, achieved and died.

Ñānavira started to beg for his food and meditate for fourteen hours a day! He was more than six feet tall, with a handsome figure, like a statue of the Buddha. My striking memory is the *metta* in his eyes and *satisampajanna* in everything he did. There was nothing that he wanted whenever I asked him, except medicine for his illness, though I once saw him writing with a pencil stub about one inch long. His mother came to take home her only son because she was lonely after the father died, and when he refused, she flew home and died in two weeks. He was twice brought to Colombo to syringe mud from his ears from bathing in muddy water at the culvert and for swelling of the knee joints from relentless *anapanasati* on a hard cement floor. The villagers regarded him as their own living god and took his *dana* to the *kuti* by sharing the days between them.

Ñāṇavira Thera attained *sotapatti* and *phala* on 27 June 1959 and wrote a letter in Pali, sealed it, "To be opened after my death" and sent to the senior monk at the Island Hermitage. These books, he later wrote, contain the Buddha's Teaching; they can be trusted absolutely from beginning to end: (*Vinayapitaka:*) Suttavibhnaga, Mahavagga, Culavagga; (*Suttapitaka:*) Dighanikaya, Majjimanikaya, Samyuttanikaya, Anguttaranikaya, Suttanipata, Dhammpada, Udana, Itivuttaka, Theratherigatha. No other book whatsoever can be trusted. Leaving aside Vinaya seek the meaning of these in your own experience. Do not seek their meaning in any other books: if you do you will be misled. He rejected the *Abhidhammapitaka*, the commentaries and texts as "leaving less to be unlearned" and also as not being the words of the Buddha.

The letter was opened in 1964, one year before he took his own life. He inhaled from a vial of ethyl chloride my mother had supplied after he used one I gave him to use as a local anesthetic for inflamed painful insect bites. He anesthetised himself by wearing an ingenious handmade cellophane facemask. When found by a villager who went with the afternoon *gilampasa*, Ñāṇavira Thera was dead, sleeping in the lion's pose, one hand fallen beside the empty vial gently laid on the floor. He died on 5 July 1965 at the age of forty-four years. Photographs taken one year before and an eyewitness Venerable Ñāṇasumana tells, "He is an old man of 60 years. He is in constant physical pain but never shows it nor does the peace in his eyes ever change. We spend many hours talking—rather he speaks and I learn". The entire village mourned. They built a pyre eight feet high. The women gave their best sarees to drape it and interned his ashes by the *kuti*, beside his empty sanctuary by the sea. Thus ended the life of a genius. But the wild elephants yet guard his *kuti*. No serpent ever harmed him. They would uncoil, move away and watch him pass. Ñāṇavira Thera is the legend of Bundala.

Ñāṇavira Thera used his linguistic skills and disciplined thinking to write on the Dhamma when he found that he could not proceed to *arahatta*. With no hope of Nibbana here and now, unable to practise intense *samadhi*, condemned to a life sentence of pain and distraction, poisoned by the medicine he was given, he wrote, "The only thing I take seriously is the Dhamma. If I cannot practise it as I want, I have no further wish to live". He rejected a suggestion to disrobe, as it is regarded as death, in the Dhamma. "No one," he wrote, "has become *arahat* in the act of disrobing." Jealous persons, who cannot get within a mile of him and of the path, mislead that Ñānavira Thera could not have understood the Dhamma—as if *arahats* who took the knife in the time of the Buddha also failed to understand it. Or, that the dialogues of Socrates have no value because he drank poison rather than escape as his friends arranged.

The truth is in the only book he wrote, *Notes on Dhamma*, 250 copies of which were cyclostyled by Lionel Samaratunga, High Court Judge, Balapitiya in 1964. The brilliance of Nanavira Thera comes alive to us now when his writings are scrutinised in the expanded book *Clearing the Path* published in 1987 by the American samanera Bodhesako with assistance from the Department for Creative Writing, University of Colorado. He included 150 selected letters Ñānavira Thera wrote to readers who asked to explain items in the *Notes* ... In Europe, it was called "the most important book of the century", and Ñānavira became a cult figure.

Clearing the Path is a difficult book no less than the Suttas. There are many western classical quotations, aphorisms, wit and humour written mainly to an elite familiar with writings of Huxley, Joyce, Satre, Kierkegaard, Kafka, Nietzche and others of that genre. He uses his mathematical and analytical skills, the laws of thought and logic to demolish comparisons of the Dhamma with quantum mechanics and with the writings of scientists quoted by some people to offer character certificates to the Buddha. He laments that people and even monks in Ceylon do not read the Suttas and are ignorant of what the Buddha actually taught. The European he says, has excess of *panna* over *saddha* and tends to reject things even when true while the Asian with excess of *saddha* over *panna* accepts things even when false. He has severely criticised by well-known scholars such as Rhys Davids, Wijesekera, and Jayatilelke who hopelessly misconstrue the teaching of the Buddha.

Ñānavira Thera has given unique, precise interpretations of selected core of the Dhamma such as *paticcasumuppada, sankhara, cetana, atta, upadana, namarupa, vinnana, avijja, phassa, the tilakkhana,* and demolished hallowed traditional books such as Milindapanha and Visuddhimagga. The unbiased intelligent reader with a compelling personal reason to study and practise the

Dhamma is invited to accept his point of view. *Clearing the Path* is out of print and I arranged to publish it in its separate parts by photographing the original. Venerable Ñānavira Thera wrote, "my aim is to clear dead matter that is choking the Suttas and if I do not write it, no one else will". The book is translated to Dutch and Serbian and is on the Internet.

VENERABLE ÑĀNAMOLI THERA (1905-60)

Osbert Moore was born in England in 1905 and graduated from Exeter College, Oxford. He was a scholar of English and French classics. Osbert was Head of the Italian section of the BBC at Bush House, London when, in the last World War, he joined the British Army Secret Service and served in Italy to interrogate prisoners of war, along with Harold Musson. (At the BBC, Moore was senior to Todd, who in the 1940s set up the Commercial Service of Radio Ceylon). After the War, he returned to his job at the BBC. He came to Sri Lanka in 1948 with Harold Musson and was ordained as Ñānamoli by Nyanatiloka Maha Thera, the (German) High Priest of the Island Hermitage, Dodanduwa, Galle in the following year.

One day, after the war, he met Harold at a pub in London and they had a long discussion till it closed, about post-War life and the purposelessness of existence. Harold persuaded him to travel together to Ceylon and assess if there was meaning for them in the words of the Buddha. He resigned from the BBC and on the way, they spent three months at an ashram of the Ramakrishna Mission in the Himalayas exploring *jhana* meditation. Dissatisfied, they came to Sri Lanka and straightaway went to Vajiraramaya temple at Bambalapitiya. They met Prof. G P Malalasekera who sent them to the Island Hermitage. After about three months as an *upasaka* learning Pali from Nyanatiloka Maha Thera, Moore and Musson were ordained at the Island Hermitage at a grand ceremony conducted by the *Sasanadhara Kantha Samitiya*, the caretakers of the hermitage. [The secretary and founder of the society was my mother Clara Heendeniya, and its Patron, when she died at the age of ninety.]

Ñānamoli Thera was a well-built, healthy, soft-spoken person with a self-effacing endearing humour. He never spoke until addressed. From the time he arrived at the hermitage he committed himself to letter all the instructions of the Buddha, devoting entirely to the study and practice of the Dhamma in seclusion in his *kuti*. It was built as designed by Ñānavira Thera, with a corridor for walking meditation leading to a small room at the end, in the shape of an L.

Ñānamoli Thera never left the hermitage until he did what he wanted to achieve. When he completed his *magnum opus*, the translation of the *Visuddhimagga*, he decided to go on a pilgrimage to Yapahuwa with the then chief monk, Nanaloka Thera, the Sinhala personal attendant of Nyanatiloka Maha Thera who had by then died. At the Fort Railway Station, my father put them in the train because none of the hermitage monks handled money. He asked, "Sir, when are you returning?" Nanamoli replied with his characteristic smile, "Bertie, how do you know I am returning?" He died from a heart attack on a lonely dust road in the backwoods of Kurunegala, about twenty-five years after walking on the lush carpets of the BBC in London. Villagers took the body to hospital in a bullock cart. The funeral was held in Colombo. Before leaving on pilgrimage, he wrote to his friend Ñānavira Thera, at Bundala, the instructions to dispose of his personal things. Venerable Ñānamoli Thera knew, perhaps from penetration of the Dhamma, that the time had come to another *bhava*.

[The two biographical sketches are from a contribution by the author to the official Sinhala Encyclopaedia, at the invitation of its Editor-in-Chief.]